CX MasterBytes

A LEADER'S HANDBOOK

SHEENA JOSEPH

ISBN 979-8-89363-968-1

Index

Experience Bytes

Product Bytes

Industry, Customer, Segment Bytes

People Bytes

Process Bytes

Technology Bytes

Decision Guides

Closing Remarks

A Note from Sheena

Greetings, dear readers, and a warm welcome to CX MasterBytes, a leader's handbook that encompasses the evolving nature of customer experience. As I sit down to pen this introductory message for you, I hope that you will find the diverse bytes on customer experience as useful in your career as I did when I learned about them.

CX MasterBytes is not just a book; it's a testament to the power of shared knowledge and collective growth in customer experience. It is intended to serve as a foundational resource for CX enthusiasts and budding professionals alike, regardless of your role — whether you're a business leader, a marketing guru, a tech wizard, or a finance whiz across any other industry or role whether a fresher, individual contributor, manager, or leader.

Throughout my career, I've come to understand, like you who have picked up this book, that CX is more than just a job. It's a calling that requires passion, dedication, and a deep understanding of both the heart and mind of the customer, with the knowledge of technology to elevate it.

With the CX MasterBytes series, I aim to share invaluable learnings gained from navigating through the myriad challenges of CX every year, drawing from the depths of the trenches to unearthing strategies for creating meaningful customer interactions.

Alongside various practical insights and actionable advice, you'll sometimes also find a sprinkle of humour woven throughout these pages. After all, laughter is not only good for our souls but also an essential key to maintaining perspective in the face of life's challenges.

With a new MasterBytes volume of CX set to be released every year, there will always be more insights, more wisdom, and more opportunities for growth on the horizon.

So, let this book be your trusted companion, guiding you toward continued success and innovation in the dynamic world of customer experience.

Warmest regards,
Sheena
Author, CX MasterBytes

An Introduction

Sheena is a seasoned leader in the telecommunications industry, having led large diverse teams for customer service in India and globally. With a multi-faceted portfolio covering all areas of operations, she has overseen over 100 product portfolios across various customer segments, driving strategic initiatives to enhance customer experience and revenue growth.

With 25 years of extensive experience, Sheena has honed her expertise in customer management and B2B operations across various esteemed organisations, including Reliance, Tata, and Birla Group companies – some of the biggest business houses in India. Her rich background encompasses leadership roles in service operations, strategy formulation, and business management, where she has consistently delivered industry benchmarks and steered successful product launches and lifecycle operations.

Sheena's expertise extends across diverse Enterprise product lines, including Mobility, IoT, Wireline Data & Voice, Cloud, Security, Managed Services, SaaS UCaaS, CCaas, and Colocation. With a reputed customer-centric approach and a track record of delivering results, she has led her teams to achieve sustainable operational excellence that has resulted in industry recognition for her efforts.

As a key leadership member in her various roles, Sheena has also played a pivotal role in shaping the strategic direction of her businesses and driving growth initiatives to meet and exceed revenue targets. Her industry knowledge and strategic vision position her as a trusted leader in the telecom sector.

Outside work and family, she is a keen follower/commentator of global technology trends and innovations that are shaping the future of businesses and society. She also shares learnings on gender inclusivity and leadership on various platforms.

A Note on How to Use CX MasterBytes

CX MasterBytes is a compass that is divided into the following section bytes with sub-bytes that form the compass for you. Happy reading!

Experience Bytes: Use the sub-bytes to immerse yourself in the world of customer experiences and understand how each interaction contributes to people's overall perception of your brand. Make it a compass that guides you while crafting experiences.

Product Bytes: Use the sub-bytes to explore the intricate details of product offerings and how they impact customer experiences. Make it a compass to guide you through the landscape of product-centric CX strategies.

Industry, Customer, and Segment Bytes: Use the sub-bytes to gain insight into industry trends, customer preferences, and segment-specific nuances, empowering you to tailor CX effectively. Make it a compass to guide you through sectional landscapes for CX strategies.

People Bytes: Use the sub-bytes to explore human roles in CX and recognise the pivotal role of employees and leaders in delivering exceptional experiences. Use this advice as a compass to help people make choices about your CX journey deliverables.

Process Bytes: Use the sub-bytes to navigate the intricacies of operational processes and workflows, optimise customer interactions, and drive organisational efficiency. This can be your compass for understanding seamless CX.

Technology Bytes: Use the sub-bytes to embrace the transformative power of technology in CX and leverage tools and solutions to enhance customer engagement and satisfaction. Let this be a compass for your digital CX.

Decision Bytes: Use the sub-bytes as a compass to guide you through the complex terrain of CX decision making and empower you to chart a course toward customer-centric success.

Experience Bytes

Your Best Shot Every Year!

Whenever the most extreme weeks of the year subside with the end of the financial year, and the intensity of the last overs of a cricket match or the dying moments of an NFL game that it resembled gets done with, it's usually time for reflections of our best shots - it is also the right reaffirmation time of the universal best shot, that CX is not just a department but an attitude that transcends all roles, hierarchies, and titles. It is never clearer than when we review the year in full, that the best CX relationships are the ones that bring the best business or best money in.

I have always believed that CX is an attitude, a mindset ingrained in every interaction, decision, and initiative we undertake, and it has the potential to take an organisation from good to great.

- As *business leaders*, our strategic decisions set the tone for the organisation's CX journey. By prioritising customer-centricity and fostering a culture of empathy and accountability, we pave the way for sustainable growth and customer loyalty.
- As *finance* leaders, our meticulous attention to detail and financial prudence directly influence the resources allocated to CX initiatives. By investing wisely in customer-centric strategies, we ensure long-term profitability and sustainable business success.
- As *marketing leaders*, our ability to communicate the value proposition and brand promise shapes customers' perceptions and expectations. By crafting compelling narratives and delivering on our brand promises, we cultivate trust and loyalty among your audience.

– As *IT leaders*, our expertise in technology and innovation enables seamless digital experiences and operational efficiencies. By leveraging cutting-edge technologies and optimising digital touchpoints, we enhance the overall customer journey and drive competitive advantage.

So here are some timeless quotes to guide you as we begin every year or month.

1. "Customer experience is not a department; it's everyone's job." - Unknown
2. "CX is not a function, it's a culture." - Forbes
3. "Customer experience is not just about what happens at the frontline; it's about the collective effort of the entire organisation." - Unknown
4. "CX is not a line item, it's the bottom line." - Unknown
5. "Customer experience is not a destination; it's a journey that involves every employee and every interaction." - Unknown
6. "In a world of constant change, customer experience is the one thing that remains consistent." - Unknown
7. "CX is not a one-time transaction; it's an ongoing relationship built on trust and loyalty." - Unknown
8. "Customer experience is not a task; it's a mindset that shapes every decision and action." - Unknown
9. "CX is not a buzzword; it's the heartbeat of successful organisations." - Unknown
10. "Customer experience is not a side dish; it's the main course that keeps customers coming back for more." - Unknown

May you keep firing your best shots every year!

Them and Us

In the field of business, customer experience (CX) can become a mission and vision for successful companies. When it does, it can be a powerful catalyst for driving growth, fostering loyalty, and propelling organisations to new heights of success. Read on to explore some famous case studies that showcase the transformative impact of CX on business growth, aligned with their mission and vision:

Amazon

Case Study: Amazon's obsession with customer satisfaction has been central to its meteoric rise. By prioritising customer convenience, personalised recommendations, and frictionless transactions, Amazon has become synonymous with e-commerce excellence, consistently outpacing competitors and capturing market share.

Mission: "To be Earth's most customer-centric company, where customers can find and discover anything they might want to buy online."

Vision: "To build a place where people can come to find and discover anything they might want to buy online."

Apple

Case Study: Apple's unwavering commitment to CX has fuelled its iconic brand loyalty and cult-like following. From intuitive product design to seamless integration across devices and exceptional customer service, Apple has created an ecosystem that delights customers and drives repeat purchases, driving sustained revenue growth.

Mission: "To bring the best user experience to its customers through its innovative hardware, software, and services."

Vision: "To create revolutionary products that enrich people's lives."

Zappos

Case Study: Zappos has revolutionised online retail by prioritising customer service above all else. Through its legendary WOW philosophy and a relentless focus on delivering exceptional experiences, Zappos has cultivated a fiercely loyal customer base, resulting in exponential revenue growth and industry recognition.

Mission: "To provide the best customer service possible and deliver WOW through service."

Vision: "To be the company that inspires the world by showing it's possible to simultaneously deliver happiness to customers, employees, vendors, shareholders, and the community in a long-term, sustainable way."

Starbucks

Case Study: Starbucks has transformed coffee culture by prioritising customer engagement, community-building, and product innovation. By creating inviting spaces, personalised rewards programmes, and memorable in-store experiences, Starbucks has cultivated a loyal customer base and expanded its global footprint, driving revenue growth year after year.

Mission: "To inspire and nurture the human spirit – one person, one cup, and one neighbourhood at a time."

Vision: "To create a culture of warmth and belonging, where everyone is welcome."

Ritz-Carlton

Case Study: Ritz-Carlton has set the gold standard for luxury hospitality by delivering personalised, memorable experiences that exceed guest expectations. Through its legendary service culture, attention to detail, and commitment to excellence, Ritz-Carlton has built a global reputation for unparalleled luxury, driving revenue growth and brand prestige.

Mission: "To provide genuine care and comfort to our guests."

Vision: "To be the premier worldwide provider of luxury experiences."

Southwest Airlines

Case Study: Southwest Airlines revolutionised the airline industry by prioritising CX and offering a unique combination of low fares, friendly service, and operational efficiency. By focusing on customer-centric values such as simplicity, reliability, and flexibility, Southwest built a loyal customer base and achieved sustained profitability, even during turbulent times in the aviation industry.

Mission: "To connect people to what's important in their lives through friendly, reliable, and low-cost air travel."

Vision: "To become the world's most loved, most flown, and most profitable airline."

JetBlue Airways

Case Study: JetBlue Airways disrupted the airline industry with its "Customer Bill of Rights" and commitment to providing a superior travel experience. By offering amenities such as comfortable seating, free snacks, and in-flight entertainment, JetBlue redefined customer expectations and set a new standard for excellence in the industry. Through its customer-centric approach, JetBlue has earned a reputation for reliability, transparency, and exceptional service, driving customer loyalty and business growth.

Mission: "To inspire humanity – both in the air and on the ground."

Vision: "To become America's favourite airline, known for its superior customer service and hospitality."

These case studies illustrate the transformative power of CX in driving business growth, fostering brand loyalty, and creating lasting value for customers and organisations alike.

These companies have also embedded CX into their DNA, with mission and vision statements that prioritise customer-centricity, innovation, and excellence.

By staying true to their core values, they continue to set the standard for CX excellence globally, earning the trust and loyalty of customers around the world.

By prioritising CX initiatives that delight customers, drive loyalty, and differentiate brands in the marketplace, businesses can unlock new opportunities for growth and success in an increasingly customer-centric world.

Let's draw inspiration from these CX success stories and embark on our journey towards business growth through customer experience excellence!

Living Roots

Organisational structures are like these manmade Living Root bridges found in Meghalaya, built over time to cement the foundations of customer service. Read on to learn how various organisational designs can elevate customer service.

Having worked across different structures in the same or different organisations, I can truly say that there is never any one-size-fits-all type of structure, and it depends on the time and market situation in a structure that remains relevant. Each organisational structure brings its unique strengths to the realm of customer service. The key lies in aligning the chosen structure with the company's values, goals, and the nature of customer interactions.

Hierarchy Structure: In a traditional hierarchy, clear reporting lines promote consistency and stability. Customer service teams follow defined processes, ensuring that inquiries are channelled efficiently. Supervisory levels facilitate problem escalation, ensuring swift resolution.

Matrix Structure: A matrix blends functional departments with project-based teams. For customer service, this means bringing diverse expertise to address complex issues. Collaboration across verticals helps tackle challenges from different angles, delivering comprehensive solutions.

Functional Structure: Organising teams based on functions ensures specialisation. Customer service benefits from experts dedicated to specific aspects, such as technical support or order fulfilment. This specialisation breeds efficiency and in-depth problem-solving.

Flat Structure: A flat structure promotes open communication and empowers team members. In customer service, this translates to direct interaction between representatives and decision-makers. Quick decisions and a sense of ownership enhance the overall service experience.

Network Structure: Networks encourage collaboration between semi-autonomous units. In customer service, this can mean decentralised service hubs, allowing local teams to cater to regional needs swiftly. Centralised coordination ensures consistency across locations.

The heart of exceptional customer service beats within the framework of an organisation's structure. Different structures provide unique avenues to champion customer-centricity.

The grass may seem greener on the other side when you leave an organisation, but each structure brings advantages and disadvantages to CX that can make or break an organisation.

The Tenets

The six tenets of customer experience are constant across industries. Having worked or interned in Hospitality, Telecom & BFSI, I can confidently state that CX can have different flavours, but similar ingredients.

Different Flavours:

BFSI: Service orbits around financial security, expertise & trust

1. Tailored Financial Guidance: Providing customised financial advice and solutions to guide customers toward their financial goals.
2. Regulatory Expertise: Navigating complex financial regulations and ensuring compliance while serving customers' needs.
3. Discreet Transactions: Safeguarding customer information & ensuring secure transactions in an evolving digital world.

Telecom: Service thrives on connectivity, technical know-how & seamless communication.

1. Technical Troubleshooting: Diagnosing and resolving network issues, connectivity concerns, and device-related queries.
2. Plan Personalisation: Offering tailored data plans, device options, and subscription packages to match diverse customer needs.
3. Network Resilience: Ensuring uninterrupted network connectivity, especially in emergencies.

Hospitality: Service is memorable experiences through warmth, attention & anticipation:

1. Personalised Welcomes: Providing warm greetings, personalised service, and anticipating guest preferences.
2. Problem Resolution: Addressing guest concerns promptly, turning challenges into opportunities to impress.
3. Creating Ambiance: Designing captivating atmospheres that evoke emotions, leaving lasting memories.

Similar Ingredients:

Empathy: Whether it's handling financial concerns in BFSI, troubleshooting connectivity issues in telecom, or ensuring comfort in hospitality, empathy forms the foundation.

Speed: In the fast-paced world of BFSI, Telecom, or the welcoming realm of hospitality, timely responses hold immense significance. Swift assistance, whether it's resolving financial queries, technical hiccups, or guest requests, cultivates trust.

Communication: Be it explaining intricate financial terms, guiding through technology nuances, or creating a welcoming atmosphere, clear and compassionate communication is paramount.

Problem-Solving: The ability to analyse situations, offer solutions, and guide customers through complexities stands tall in BFSI, Telecom, and hospitality alike.

Exceeding Expectations: The enchantment of customer service lies in going above and beyond. Be it the surprise touch in BFSI, the personalised solution in Telecom, or the thoughtful gesture in Hospitality, it leaves a lasting impact.

Feedback: Every industry thrives on customer feedback. Adapting based on customer input enhances service quality, whether it's financial offerings, connectivity solutions, or guest experiences.

The aim is always to keep customers returning for more.

Winners

Price vs. Quality: Which Matters Most to You?

It's the shopping season, a time when we face the age-old dilemma of choosing between brands—one known for offering budget-friendly prices and the other renowned for top-notch service quality. Here is a tale on the same.

The Price of Excellence: A Tale of Service Quality

Once upon a time in the bustling city of Customerburg, there was a family-owned restaurant called "Fine Bites." It was renowned for its exceptional service quality, where every detail was perfected to create memorable dining experiences.

On the other side of town was a chain of fast-food joints called "Quick Grub." Quick Grub offered budget-friendly meals, but the service was often hurried and impersonal.

Now, meet my protagonist, Sanjay. He was known in Customerburg for his love of food and also for his quest to save money. Sanjay decided to compare these two establishments, "Fine Bites" and "Quick Grub."

Round 1: Dining at Fine Bites

Sanjay entered Fine Bites, where the ambiance was warm, and the staff greeted him with genuine smiles. He noticed the menu was filled with delightful dishes and decided to try a chef's special. The food arrived hot and beautifully presented. The waiter was attentive, ensuring his glass was never empty. The chef even came out to ask how he enjoyed the meal. Sanjay left Fine Bites with a full stomach and a smile, even though he had spent more than he initially planned.

Round 2: Grabbing a Quick Meal at Quick Grub

A few days later, Sanjay visited Quick Grub. He ordered a valuable meal, paid quickly at the counter, and got his food within minutes. The taste was decent, but the experience was forgettable. No one asked about his satisfaction, and he left without any interaction with the staff.

The Verdict: Price vs. Quality

Sanjay couldn't help but ponder over his experiences. At Fine Bites, he had paid more but left with an enriched memory. At Quick Grub, he saved some bucks but couldn't recall anything noteworthy.

The moral of this story is clear: In the world of CX, you often get what you pay for.

But, while price is a crucial consideration, it's not the only factor. Service quality can make a significant difference in the experiences we cherish and remember.

Striking a Perfect Chord:

So, how do you choose between service quality and price? The answer is not a one-size-fits-all formula but a personalised journey. It's about understanding your needs, values, and priorities. Sometimes, it means investing in a quality gadget that will stand the test of time. Other times, it might be choosing the pocket-friendly airline for a quick weekend getaway.

In the end, the balance you find between service quality and price is as unique as your fingerprint. It's about making informed decisions that align with your preferences, ensuring that you derive maximum value and satisfaction from your choices.

I Apologise

"I apologise for the inconvenience caused" is a common rote statement at most call centres. The particular script is expected to show servility and humility in CX, but it's one that displeases most due to a lack of authenticity at times. In the myriad of interactions in customer experience, the true winner is the one who can elegantly be of service without surrendering authenticity - to put it in a nutshell, being of service is better than being only servile.

The difference between being servile and being of service is the balance between meeting expectations and maintaining the integrity of the service provided.

Being Servile:

Imagine a scenario where a customer, albeit mistaken, demands the moon. The servile approach might involve endless apologies, compliance without question, and an unwavering 'customer is always right' stance. It's akin to bending so much that you risk breaking.

Being of Service:

Contrastingly, being of service is a nuanced art. It involves understanding the customer's needs, even when they may not fully grasp them. Instead of blind compliance, it's about guiding the customer toward a resolution. It's a balance of empathy, assertiveness, and genuine problem-solving.

Examples:

Being Servile: Apologising profusely even when the customer's demand is beyond reason, leading to potential overcommitment and dissatisfaction.

Being of Service: Acknowledging the customer's concerns, providing clarity on policies, and proposing a reasonable solution, fostering a healthier and more sustainable relationship.

Being of service involves a more dynamic, empathetic exchange. It's not about subservient acquiescence but a display of mutual respect. Conversely, servility might seem accommodating, but it lacks the depth of genuine service.

In a true customer-centric world, it is the mix of authenticity and assertiveness that creates a harmonious CX.

Ring Out

"Ring out the Old and Ring in the New" is a poem by Alfred Tennyson written for a new year, but easily applicable to corporate life and CX when you must work on burying outdated notions. Customer service, like fashion trends or viral memes, has its fair share of outdated notions. It's high time we bid adieu to these relics of the past and make room for a fresh, customer-centric approach.

Here are twelve outdated notions:

1. *"Service Is Someone Else's Job:"*

Service is everyone's job. It's a company-wide responsibility.

2. *"One-Size-Fits-All Service:"*

In the era of personalisation, treating all customers the same is a grave mistake. Your customers are unique; your service should be, too.

3. *"Customer Feedback Is a Suggestion Box:"*

Feedback is not just for show. It's a goldmine of insights. Don't treat it like an old suggestion box hidden in the corner.

4. *"Scripted Interactions Are Best:"*

Reading from a script might be safe, but it's also painfully dull. Customers appreciate genuine, human conversations.

5. *"The Customer's Role Is to Be Silent:"*

Customers have voices; let them sing their praises or vent their frustrations. Engage with them in a dialogue.

6. *"Complaints Are Bad for Business:"*

Complaints are your hidden allies. Embrace them. They point out flaws you can fix to keep your customers happy.

7. *"Service Stops at Closing Time:"*

In the digital age, service never sleeps. The 24/7 model is the way to go.

8. *"Customer Loyalty Is a Given:"*

Don't take loyalty for granted. You must earn it, day by day, interaction by interaction.

9. *"Service Is a Cost Centre:"*

Service is an investment, not an expense. It can drive revenue, build loyalty, and create brand advocates.

10. *"The Customer's Memory Is Short:"*

With the internet at their fingertips, customers remember everything. Deliver consistently great service.

11. *"Keeping Up with Technology Is Optional:"*

In the digital age, embracing the latest technology is not just beneficial; it's essential.

12. *"CX Is Only for B2C Companies:"*

CX (customer experience) is for everyone, including B2B. Every customer deserves a great experience.

It's time to toss these outdated notions into the dustbin of history and embrace a modern, customer-centric mindset. In the world of customer service too, change is the only constant.

Soaring

Technology can enable the evolution from transactional to transformative customer service and thus help soar to heights like paragliding. Read on to learn how to soar customer support in four stages:

From Reactive
to Proactive
to Predictive
to Pre-emptive

Which stage of the journey are you at?

Reactive Support: This is the traditional 'break-fix' approach. Customer issues are addressed as they arise. For instance, a customer experiencing a technical glitch in their software reaches out to support, and the team works to resolve the issue promptly. While reactive support solves immediate problems, it's more about responding to issues than preventing them.

Tech Enablers: Ticketing Systems, CRM Software

Proactive Support: In this approach, the support team anticipates potential issues and reaches out to customers before they encounter problems. Technology turns anticipation into action. AI-powered analytics and customer behaviour tracking help identify trends and patterns. Automated emails, push notifications, and chatbots engage customers before problems occur, ensuring they feel valued and attended to.

Tech Enablers: AI Analytics, Automation Tools, Chatbots

Predictive Support: Here, data analytics plays a key role. By analysing past behaviour and trends, the support team predicts potential issues and reaches out to customers with solutions before they're aware of the problem. Big data and machine learning take centre stage. Algorithms analyse historical data to predict potential issues. This enables support teams to pre-emptively address concerns before they escalate, creating a seamless customer experience.

Tech Enablers: Machine Learning, Data Analytics, Predictive Models

Pre-emptive Support: This takes customer support to the next level by preventing problems before they even surface. It involves leveraging advanced technology like AI and machine learning to anticipate issues and take preventive actions. Smart devices, sensors, and AI algorithms work together to detect anomalies and take preventive actions. This not only averts problems but elevates service to a level of anticipation customers truly appreciate.

Tech Enablers: AI, IoT Devices, Predictive Algorithms

Each level of customer support adds a layer of value and sophistication, ranging from resolving immediate issues to anticipating and preventing problems altogether. By adopting a mix of these approaches, businesses can cater to diverse customer needs and build lasting relationships that go beyond basic transactions.

The takeaway is also that it is imperative to remember that the goal is to create seamless and delightful experiences that go beyond simple issue resolution and not just use the technology itself.

Codes of Honour

In CX, there exists a set of cheat codes that, when applied strategically to differentiate service, can level up your customer experience game in any industry. Let's unveil the steps that blend customer segmentation, lifecycle elements, and the integration of people, processes, and tools.

Cheat Code Step 1: Customer Segmentation Mastery

- Parameters like product usage, revenue contribution, market penetration, and growth potential become the compass for customer segmentation.
- Determine distinct customer segments that align with your business goals and are ripe for tailored service differentiation.

Cheat Code Step 2: Lifecycle Element Differentiation

- Analyse the customer journey to pinpoint pivotal lifecycle elements.
- Differentiate elements based on each segment's unique needs. For example, high-value customers might crave personalised onboarding, while potential growth segments may benefit from targeted educational resources.

Cheat Code Step 3: Leveraging the Pillars: People, Processes, Tools

People - Your Skilled Avatars:

Objective: Assemble Your Dream Team

- Assign skilled individuals to each customer segment. Tailor training programmes to equip them with the specific skills needed for their segment.
- Cultivate a customer-centric mindset across your teams, making them empathetic avatars attuned to the nuances of each player type.

Processes - Crafting Your Experiences:

Objective: Design Seamless Interactions

- Engineer processes that align with the differentiated lifecycle elements.
- Create flexible workflows that adapt to the unique requirements of each customer segment, ensuring a seamless and personalised service journey.

Tools - Your Magical Artefacts:

Objective: Equip Your Champions

- Invest in tools that amplify the strengths of your service differentiation strategy.
- Leverage advanced analytics for segment-specific insights, communication tools for personalised interactions, and automation for streamlined processes.

Cheat Code Step 4: Measurement & Iteration

- Establish key performance indicators (KPIs) aligned with your service differentiation goals.
- Regularly measure and analyse the performance of your strategy against these KPIs.
- Iterate based on insights, adapting your cheat codes for an evolving and ever-improving service differentiation strategy.

The Grand Prize: Customer Delight & Loyalty:

- Successfully applying these cheat codes unlocks the ultimate reward – delight and unwavering loyalty.
- Loyal customers become your brand advocates, contributing to sustained growth and success.

Mastering the intricacies of customer segmentation, lifecycle element differentiation, and the strategic use of people, processes, and tools can position your brand as a true player known for exceptional CX.

Adipoli

Can you turn a mistake into a moment of magic for customers and get an **'adipoli'** (awesome in the Malayalam language) from them? Here are six well-known trend-setting service recovery examples from telecom. Turning an oops into an outstanding is the essence of the art of service recovery and can be an opportunity that helps strengthen customer relationships.

Remember, in the unpredictable journey of customer service, even the best of us can hit a bump or two. It's about how you navigate them, rather than just avoiding them.

Verizon's Bill Transparency: Verizon realised that complex billing statements frustrated customers. In response, they simplified their bills and introduced a "Bill Explanation" feature, allowing customers to understand charges better and reducing billing-related complaints.

T-Mobile's 'Team of Experts:' T-Mobile introduced its 'Team of Experts' customer service model, where customers are connected directly to a dedicated team. This personal touch and quick problem resolution have won over many frustrated customers from other carriers.

AT&T's HBO Bonanza: AT&T's streaming service, HBO Max, faced a rocky launch. To make amends, AT&T offered free HBO Max subscriptions to many of its wireless customers, turning a service issue into a perk that delighted subscribers.

Virgin Media's 'Red Door:' Virgin Media faced a widespread service outage. To apologise, they created a heartwarming ad featuring a young girl's red door, which became a symbol of the company's commitment to fixing the issue. Customers appreciated the transparent approach.

BT's Fibre Compensation: BT Openreach, part of BT Group, compensated customers for missed appointments or delayed installations. They pledged to pay £25 for every missed appointment and £5 for every day a customer's broadband service was delayed. This approach ensured accountability.

Vodafone's Global Roaming Resolution: Vodafone faced criticism over roaming charges for customers travelling outside the EU. They responded by introducing 'Vodafone Global Roaming,' offering inclusive roaming in more destinations, thus addressing a major pain point.

The most loyal customers are often the ones who experienced a service issue and saw how you handled it!

Talk to Me

Can you call a customer 'Night Owl' for surfing late hours? Yes, said Marketing. No, said the Service folks. Depends on the context, said the wise old person. Service Communication can be a successful service strategy that aids experiences. Here is a snippet on why Service Communication, Marketing Communication, and Employee communication are different skill sets, while themed around the art of communication.

On a light note:

Marketing communication is the stage announcer, shouting about the world's best funnel cakes. Their mission? Attract and seduce potential customers into the Big Top of Buying.

Employee communication is backstage whisperers, making sure everyone's in sync with a script, even if it's casual Friday's Hawaiian shirt competition.

Service Communication are the firefighters of the corporate circus. When things go awry, they put out fires, save the day, and even crack a joke or two to keep everyone smiling.

But seriously,

Service Communication:

At the heart lies the customer experience

Focus: It revolves around addressing customer inquiries, resolving issues, and providing support. It's all about assisting customers with empathy in communication.

Interaction: It's a two-way street where businesses engage with customers to understand needs, offer solutions, and maintain lasting relationships.

Personalisation: Tailoring responses and solutions to individual customer situations is key. The aim is to create personalised interactions that resonate with the customer's concerns.

Marketing Communication:

At the heart, it paints the brand's canvas inviting customers to join the story.

Objective: The goal is to create awareness, generate interest, and prompt action, such as making a purchase. Marketing communication focuses on presenting the brand in its best light.

Broadcast: It's a broadcast approach, reaching a broader audience with compelling messages that evoke emotions and prompt them to take specific actions.

Brand Storytelling: Weaves narratives around the brand's values, products, and services to foster a connection and inspire brand loyalty.

Employee Communication:

At the heart, it is the organisation's heartbeat.

Internal Alignment: It aims to keep the workforce informed, aligned with company goals, and engaged in the organisation's journey.

Audience: The primary recipients are the employees. It ensures they are well-informed about company news, updates, policies, and opportunities.

Cultivating Culture: It fosters a sense of belonging, transparency, and open dialogue, creating a positive work environment that supports employee growth and satisfaction.

While these communication streams differ in their purpose and audience, they collectively contribute to the harmonious functioning of a company, and in many places, all the twain meet.

Sir/Madam

Do you have a Sir/Madam culture in your organisation? Is it merely an honorific term, a cultural tradition, or a sign of servility?

In the context of CX, a general Sir/Madam addressing culture is as outdated as a dial-up modem in today's world of fibre optics. Here's why:

The Sir/Madam Conundrum in B2B:

During interactions, the formality of 'Sir' or 'Madam' can often feel contrived and distant.

It's like wearing a tuxedo to a backyard barbecue.

Personalisation is Key: Today's CX thrives on personalisation. Customers expect you to know their name, their needs, and their quirks (well, maybe not the quirks, but you get the idea).

Robo-Responses Aren't Cool: Using these generic salutations can make your communication seem automated and robotic. Nobody wants to feel like they're chatting with a bot.

Building Relationships: B2B CX is all about building lasting relationships. Ditching the formalities in favour of a more conversational approach can set the stage for genuine connections.

And here's why it's time to reconsider this even in B2C:

The Rise of Automation: In an era of chatbots and automated responses, using formal titles like 'Sir' or 'Madam' can make interactions feel cold and impersonal. It's like talking to a machine, not a human.

Too Formal for Today: Business landscapes have evolved. We're moving away from stiff, formal interactions towards more relaxed, conversational exchanges. 'Sir' and 'Madam' can create unnecessary barriers.

Personalisation Matters: Customer experience is all about personalisation. Customers want to feel seen and understood, and that starts with using their names instead of generic titles.

It's About Conversation: Imagine you're sitting across from a client in a café. Would you start the conversation with 'Sir' or 'Madam?' Probably not. You'd jump right into the discussion.

So, it's time to bid adieu to the old-school 'Sir/Madam' and embrace authentic, engaging, and human-centric customer experiences. After all, more than titles, CX is about meaningful connections.

The Myths

While a great Aadhar photo is certainly a myth and, like the Facebook photo, may not be fact, here are ten myths to debunk about CX:

Myth 1: *Speed is Everything*

Fact: Speed matters, but rushing through service is like speed-dating – not everyone finds their perfect match in 30 seconds.

Example: Lightning-fast responses are great, but a thoughtful solution beats a hasty one.

Myth 2: *Handling Complaints is Negative*

Fact: Handling complaints well is like a superhero saving the day – it can turn unhappy customers into the biggest fans.

Example: An airline resolves a baggage issue promptly and offers compensation, turning an initially unhappy customer into a loyal, satisfied one.

Myth 3: *Customers Only Care About Price*

Fact: Customers are gourmet foodies who appreciate quality and service, not just the cheapest dish.

Example: A Michelin-starred restaurant isn't competing on price; it's about the whole experience.

Myth 4: *Automation Solves Everything*

Fact: Automation is cool, but replacing humans with robots is like having a robot comedian – the jokes might fall flat.

Example: Automated chatbots can help, but some matters need a human touch.

Myth 5: *Customers Want to Speak to a Human*

Fact: Some prefer human interaction; others are like self-checkout fans – they like doing things themselves

Example: Online banking allows customers to check balances and transfer funds without talking to a human agent

Myth 6: *Apologies Admit Fault*

Fact: Apologising is like saying 'sorry' when someone sneezes – it's a courtesy, not an admission of guilt.

Example: Apologising for inconveniences, like sneezes, without accepting blame.

Myth 7: *Good Service is Enough*

Fact: Good service is like having a cake, but exceptional service is the frosting and sprinkles.

Example: A hotel that provides a welcome gift and personalised service goes the extra mile, creating memorable experiences.

Myth 8: *It's* Too Expensive to Keep Customers

Fact: Keeping customers is like gardening – nurturing what you have is often cheaper than planting new seeds.

Example: Offering loyalty rewards is like fertilising your customer garden – it keeps them growing.

Myth 9: *You Can't Measure customer service*

Fact: Trying to measure without metrics is like trying to bake without a recipe – you're just winging it.

Example: Metrics like Net Promoter Score (NPS) give you the recipe for baking up great service.

Myth 10: *Customers Don't Notice Small Gestures*

Fact: Small gestures are like sprinkles on the service cupcake – they add a delightful touch.

Example: A coffee shop barista remembering a regular customer's preferred drink shows attention to detail and care.

Smile, You are on Camera

How do you measure a Customer's Smile and its intensity?

Measuring service experience allows us to gain valuable insights, identify areas for improvement, and ensure that we are meeting customer expectations. Here are some key metrics that help us quantify and enhance the impact of customer service!

Churn Rate and Retention Rate: The churn rate measures the percentage of customers who discontinue using our service, while the retention rate measures customer loyalty. A lower churn rate and higher retention rate indicate a successful service experience that keeps customers coming back.

Net Promoter Score (NPS): NPS gauges customer loyalty and their likelihood to recommend our service to others. By asking customers to rate on a scale of 0 to 10, we can segment them into Promoters, Passives, and Detractors. NPS helps identify brand advocates and areas that require attention.

Customer Satisfaction (CSAT): CSAT is a fundamental metric gauges customer satisfaction with a specific service interaction. Using post-interaction surveys, we can ask customers to rate their experience on a scale of 1 to 5 or 1 to 10. Analysing CSAT scores over time helps us track trends and identify patterns to optimise our service delivery.

First Contact Resolution (FCR): FCR determines the percentage of customer inquiries or problems resolved during their initial interaction with support. A high FCR rate indicates effective problem-solving and reduces the need for follow-up contacts, leading to higher customer satisfaction.

Response Time and Resolution Time: Monitoring the average response time to customer inquiries and the time taken to resolve their issues provides valuable insights into service efficiency. Prompt responses and swift resolutions contribute to positive service experiences.

Quality Assurance (QA) Assessments: QA assessments involve evaluating interactions between service representatives and customers. This can be done through call monitoring, chat transcripts, or email evaluations. QA helps maintain service quality and provides feedback for continuous improvement.

Customer Feedback and Surveys: Regularly soliciting customer feedback through surveys, focus groups, or feedback forms allows us to understand their needs, pain points, and suggestions. Customer feedback is a goldmine of insights for service enhancement.

Social Media Listening and Sentiment Analysis: Monitoring social media channels and analysing customer sentiments provide a real-time pulse of how customers perceive our service. Responding promptly to social media interactions contributes to a positive brand image.

A purely qualitative one, though, can also be effusive customer appreciation given to teams by customers. The effort taken by a customer to give such feedback is truly reflective of the experience provided.

Smiling Channels

CX requires engaging with customers across channels. Each channel has its own set of quirks, so here are some learnings with a dash of humour to lighten up.

Walk-Ins

Learning: Walk-ins are the impromptu stand-up shows of customer service. A customer strolls in, expectations in tow, and CX folks must be the lead in a sitcom trying to provide a solution while balancing coffee. Timing is everything in this live performance!

Phone Calls

Learning: Phone calls are a vocal symphony, where the voice of a CX professional is the main instrument. Navigating through technical difficulties, accents thicker than molasses, and the occasional "Can you hear me now?" can echo like a recurring chorus.

Emails

Learning: Emails are the written word ballet, where eloquence meets brevity. Crafting responses is akin to pirouettes; it's a dance between clarity and charm while avoiding the landmines of typos and accidental 'Reply All' catastrophes.

Live Chats

Learning: Live chats are the typing tango where nimble fingers lead. Speed is of the essence as a CX professional strives to outwit autocorrect, maintain the rhythm of the conversation, and occasionally throw in an emoji or two for extra flair.

Facebook

Learning: Facebook interactions are social media shenanigans, where the public eye transforms every query into a potential spectacle. Responding with wit and warmth is the key to turning a potential drama into a delightful sitcom.

Bots

Learning: Conversations with bots are encounters with a digital oracle. A surreal experience where you must decode cryptic responses to reassure customers that there is a human behind the curtain, pulling the strings to help.

Twitter

Learning: Twitter, with its 280 characters, is the stand-up comedy of customer service. Delivering punchlines with brevity, responding to a public audience, and perhaps throwing in a GIF for good measure – it's a tightrope walk of humour and conciseness.

Video Calls

Learning: Video calls are the virtual vaudeville act. With backgrounds that may reveal more than intended and occasional frozen screen frames, the challenge is to maintain professionalism while embracing the unpredictable antics of technology.

Forums

Learning: Engaging in forums is akin to performing at a community comedy club. A CX professional's responses must resonate with the diverse audience, addressing concerns while navigating a cacophony of opinions—a balancing act of diplomacy and humour.

The lessons learned are still about providing solutions and orchestrating services that leave customers smiling. So, let your interactions be filled with laughter, your responses be as witty as a stand-up routine, and may your multichannel symphony continue to entertain and delight! The positivity of looking at them humorously can help you maintain sanity in the pressure-driven world of CX.

Live & Laugh

Who doesn't enjoy a good laugh? Humour is the most potent weapon in life, and CX is used to deal with challenges or foster relationships. It can humanise a brand and make memorable interactions for customers. Here are some learnings on humour in CX connects of B2B account engagement:

Breaking the Ice with Levity:

- *Insight:* Humour is the master key that effortlessly unlocks doors in the initial stages of customer interactions. A well-placed joke or light-hearted comment serves as an icebreaker, instantly putting customers at ease and setting a positive tone for the conversation.

Fostering Genuine Connections:

- *Insight:* Laughter forms a bridge between service provider and customer, fostering a genuine connection. Shared moments of humour create an emotional bond that transcends the transactional nature of the interaction, making customers feel understood and valued.

Navigating Challenges with a Smile:

- *Insight:* When faced with challenges or complex issues, humour becomes the compass that guides the way. A touch of wit can lighten the mood, making the problem-solving process more collaborative and less daunting for all involved.

Memorability Through Laughter:

- *Insight:* The most memorable interactions are often the ones sprinkled with laughter. Incorporating humour into customer connections ensures that the brand experience stands out, leaving a lasting impression that goes beyond the specifics of the service provided.

Elevating Customer Experience:

- *Insight:* Humour has the power to elevate the entire customer experience. From witty email responses to clever social media engagements, injecting humour into various touchpoints can enhance the overall journey, making it efficient and enjoyable.

Humanising the Brand:

- *Insight:* Humour humanises the brand, breaking down the walls of formality. Customers appreciate and connect with brands that have a human touch, and humour serves as a powerful tool for showcasing the approachable and relatable side of the business.

Encouraging Open Communication:

- *Insight:* Laughter encourages open and honest communication. When customers perceive a brand as approachable and willing to share a laugh, they are more likely to express their thoughts, feedback, and concerns openly, leading to more meaningful interactions.

Strengthening Resilience:

- *Insight:* Humour is a resilient ally during challenging moments. The ability to find humour even in difficult situations not only eases tension but also demonstrates resilience and a positive outlook, attributes that customers appreciate in their service providers.

Here's to more laughter, connections, and humour in customer experiences!

Fit You

Fitness has never been more important, and you realise this as you advance in years of experience. Let's explore the symbiotic relationship between these two seemingly distinct facets of life.

Endurance and Resilience:

Fitness: Physical fitness demands endurance & resilience. Whether it's pushing through the last mile or conquering a challenging workout, resilience is the cornerstone of fitness achievements.

CX: Similarly, in CX, professionals need endurance to navigate challenges, adapt to changes, and maintain a relentless focus on enhancing experiences.

Continuous Improvement:

Fitness: The essence of fitness lies in continuous improvement. Whether it's increasing weights, refining techniques, or achieving personal milestones, the journey is a progression towards better versions of oneself.

CX: In CX, a commitment to continuous improvement is pivotal. Learning from customer feedback, optimising processes, and staying attuned to industry trends contribute to ongoing development.

Goal Setting and Achievement:

Fitness: Setting fitness goals and achieving them is a powerful motivator. Whether it's running a marathon, mastering a yoga pose, or hitting a personal record, goals drive fitness enthusiasts to strive more.

CX: In CX, goal setting is vital. Establishing benchmarks for satisfaction, retention rates, or efficiency propels one towards the collective goal of delivering outstanding experiences.

Wellness for Optimal Performance:

Fitness: Prioritising wellness is integral to peak physical performance. Adequate rest, proper nutrition, and mindfulness contribute to sustained energy and optimal fitness levels.

CX: Similarly, ensuring the wellness of a team is crucial. A positive work environment, ongoing training, and a supportive culture foster optimal performance & innovation in delivering exceptional service.

Adaptability to Change:

Fitness: Adaptability is a hallmark of fitness. From adjusting workout routines to overcoming plateaus, the ability to adapt is key to sustained progress.

CX: In the dynamic field of CX, adaptability is also vital. Responding to changing customer needs, emerging technologies, and market shifts requires a flexible & adaptive mindset.

Team Collaboration:

Fitness: Many fitness endeavours involve group activities. Team sports, fitness classes, or workout buddies highlight the significance of collaboration.

CX: CX careers thrive on collaboration. Cross-functional teamwork, effective communication, and a shared commitment to satisfaction create a collaborative environment for success.

May you always strike the balance and thrive in both the fitness arena and CX careers!

Product Bytes

The Sprint

In the sprint to stay ahead of the curve - Would you bet on Product Quality or Service Quality?

Products are what you buy, but service is what you experience, said the CX folks, of course.

In the B2B world, it is said products may keep fading, but it is CX that helps build connections and sustain them. It is indeed a captivating question:

Can a brilliant product survive a lacklustre customer experience? Conversely, can an exceptional customer experience salvage a less-than-stellar product?

When Brilliance Falls Flat: Good Product, Bad CX

Picture this: a groundbreaking product engineered to perfection, yet its brilliance falters when met with a cumbersome, frustrating customer journey. In this act, we explore the vulnerabilities of a business that underestimates the power of customer delight. It's a reminder that even the most exceptional products can wither without the nurturing embrace of a seamless customer experience.

Elevating Imperfections: Bad Product, Great CX

Now, shift the spotlight to a different scene—a stage where a product, flawed and imperfect, finds redemption through an extraordinary customer experience. Here, we delve into the alchemy of turning setbacks into triumphs. The resilience of businesses that understand the art of transforming customer interactions into moments of delight, even in the face of product shortcomings.

Decoding Long-Term Sustainability: The Balancing Act

As we ponder the question - What is more sustainable in the long run? Is it the enduring allure of a remarkable product or the staying power of a consistently excellent customer experience? The answer probably is that the relationship between product quality and service quality is symbiotic. We should continue to explore the dance between product excellence and customer-centric strategies and seek the perfect equilibrium for sustained success.

Good to Great

Every CX professional always likes to be associated with great products. Having a great product makes CX infinitely easier or sometimes even eliminates the need for a CX team because it is so sustainable by itself.

Here's a look at what makes a great product from a good product. When you recognise them, they become learning guides to building them or even help uncover opportunities in the CX for improvement in the CX space.

User-Centric Evolution:

Greatness starts with a deep understanding of user needs. A good product becomes great by continuously evolving to meet and exceed user expectations and adapting to changing behaviours and preferences.

Innovation Catalyst:

Innovation is the secret sauce. Great products embrace continuous innovation, whether through groundbreaking features, technological advancements, or creative problem-solving. It's always about staying ahead of the curve.

Seamless User Experience (UX):

The journey from good to great involves refining the user experience. Great products prioritise a seamless, intuitive UX, ensuring that every interaction is a delightful and memorable experience.

Iterative Enhancement:

The path to greatness is a journey of constant refinement. Listening to user feedback, analysing performance metrics, and iteratively enhancing features contribute to a product's ongoing evolution.

Design Distinction:

Aesthetics matter, but design excellence is more than skin deep. Great products boast a design that not only captivates visually but also aligns with functionality.

Reliability and Performance Boost:

Greatness is synonymous with reliability. Elevating a good product to greatness involves optimising performance, ensuring stability, and creating an environment where users can depend on the product consistently.

Scalability Mastery:

A great product is prepared for growth. Scalability is the key, allowing the product to handle increased demand without compromising user experience or system performance.

Sustainability Integration:

In our era of conscious consumerism, greatness involves a commitment to sustainability. Products that integrate eco-friendly practices and align with environmental values resonate more deeply with users.

Distinctive Brand Alignment:

Great products are not just features; they are brand ambassadors. Aligning the product's identity with the overarching brand narrative enhances the overall brand image, creating a powerful and cohesive story.

Adaptability to Change:

The journey from good to great includes adaptability. Great products anticipate and adapt to technological advancements and market shifts, ensuring long-term relevance.

How many of the above ten can you resonate with in a favourite product?

Horses for Courses

"Horses for Courses" is a term that refers to embracing tailored approaches for success! Having handled the lifecycle operations of close to 100 plus products, the key learning is that just as different horses excel on specific racecourses, different products require tailored service strategies. Some examples from telecom:

IoT

Customer Needs: IoT customers seek seamless connectivity, real-time monitoring, and predictive maintenance to harness the full potential of their interconnected devices. They demand data security, easy integration, and robust IoT platforms to optimise operations.

Service Strategy: Offer specialised IoT troubleshooting, proactive monitoring, and personalised support for complex IoT deployments.

Mobility

Customer Needs: Mobility customers crave instant access, frictionless experiences, and mobile-first solutions that align with their on-the-go lifestyle. They expect smooth app functionality, reliable networks, and personalised support for devices.

Service Strategy: Prioritise swift issue resolution, streamline mobile app support, and provide omnichannel assistance for seamless customer experiences. Stay ahead of mobile technology trends to empower customers with cutting-edge solutions.

Wireline: Data Connectivity

Customer Needs: Wireline customers value uninterrupted, high-speed connectivity and reliable network performance for both home and business usage. They require timely technical assistance and tailored bandwidth solutions.

Service Strategy: Invest in robust network monitoring tools, optimise troubleshooting processes, and offer flexible bandwidth options to cater to usage patterns. Provide timely communication during network maintenance to minimise disruptions.

Cloud Solutions

Customer Needs: Cloud customers demand scalable, secure, and cost-effective solutions that align with unique business requirements. They seek guidance on cloud migration, data management, and optimising cloud performance.

Service Strategy: Offer expert consultation, implement security best practices, and provide personalised guidance to ensure seamless cloud integration and management.

Data Centre Solutions

Customer Needs: Data centre customers require robust, reliable solutions to safeguard their critical data. They seek expert guidance on data centre setup, maintenance, and disaster recovery planning to ensure continuous operations.

Service Strategy: Offer comprehensive consultations on design, implement rigorous security measures, and provide proactive monitoring to safeguard customers' valuable information.

SaaS: Software as a Service Solutions

Customer Needs: SaaS customers desire user-friendly, efficient solutions that streamline their workflows. They seek regular updates, seamless integration, and reliable support to maximise productivity.

Service Strategy: Ensure regular updates and enhancements to optimise SaaS performance. Provide ongoing training and responsive support to empower customers to make the most of their SaaS experience.

Industry, Customer, Segment Bytes

1. *B&C*
2. *Connects*
3. *The Cycle*
4. *Money*
5. *Each One*

B&C

B2B vs. B2C - Understanding these five nuances can help plan your customer service strategy.

Relationship vs. Transaction:

B2B interactions are often built on long-term, strategic relationships, while B2C interactions are more transactional. B2B customer service focuses on nurturing and strengthening partnerships, understanding complex business needs, and providing solutions that drive mutual success.

In contrast, B2C customer service emphasises delivering a seamless and enjoyable experience in each transaction. It's all about building lasting relationships versus optimising individual interactions.

Complex Decision Making:

B2B purchases typically involve multiple decision-makers and complex buying processes. B2B customer service teams need to understand the intricacies of the customer's business, industry, and objectives. They must offer deep expertise, consultative guidance, and tailored solutions to address specific challenges.

On the other hand, B2C customer service focuses more on quick issue resolution, addressing individual consumer needs efficiently. It's about understanding the consumer's preferences and providing personalised support promptly.

Volume and Scale:

B2B customer service often deals with a smaller customer base but with higher transaction values and more significant account management responsibilities. B2B teams must handle complex product configurations, pricing negotiations, and ongoing support.

In contrast, B2C customer service typically faces larger customer volumes, shorter sales cycles, and a greater emphasis on mass-market interactions. It's about providing efficient, scalable solutions to accommodate a broader customer base.

Customer Expertise:

B2B customer service necessitates a deep understanding of the customer's industry, business goals, and specific challenges. B2B teams should act as trusted advisers, offering insights, strategic recommendations, and customised solutions.

In contrast, B2C customer service focuses more on product knowledge, addressing common consumer queries, and providing excellent service across various touchpoints. It's about being well-versed in the product or service and ensuring customer satisfaction at every step.

Lengthy Sales Cycles:

B2B sales cycles are typically longer, involving multiple touchpoints and stages of evaluation. B2B customer service teams play a vital role in nurturing relationships, providing ongoing support, and guiding customers through the entire sales journey.

In contrast, B2C sales cycles are often shorter, requiring prompt and efficient customer service to drive immediate purchase decisions. It's about creating memorable experiences that prompt consumer loyalty and repeat business.

The ideal service is, however, where you can build the speed of B2C with the class of B2B.

Connects

Customer satisfaction is worthless. Customer loyalty is priceless, is the golden mantra in B2B CX and every interaction is an opportunity to make a positive impact. The threads woven through meaningful customer connections are often crucibles of insights.

Here are ten short learnings distilled from some valuable B2B customer connects:

Empathy is the Bridge:

Empathy is not just a word; it's the bridge that connects the service provider with the customer. Understanding the customer's perspective, challenges, and aspirations fosters a connection that goes beyond transactions.

Listening is an Art:

Amid the rush of conversations, the art of active listening emerges as a cornerstone. Every customer interaction is an opportunity to listen intently, not just to words but to the nuances that reveal unspoken needs.

Solutions Over Transactions:

Good customer connections emphasise solutions over transactions. It's about going beyond providing a service or product; it's about addressing the underlying needs and ensuring a comprehensive solution.

Consistency Builds Trust:

Consistency in service delivery is the bedrock of trust. Whether it's the first interaction or a long-term relationship, customers appreciate reliability and a consistent commitment to excellence.

Personalisation Matters:

The era of personalisation is here to stay. Tailoring interactions based on individual preferences, history, and unique needs adds a layer of care that resonates deeply with customers.

Acknowledging Mistakes Builds Credibility:

Mistakes happen, but acknowledging them with transparency builds credibility. Customers value honesty, and admitting errors while actively working to rectify them strengthens the customer-provider bond.

Proactive Communication is Key:

The power of proactive communication cannot be overstated. Keeping customers informed about relevant updates, improvements, or potential challenges demonstrates a commitment to transparency.

Every Interaction Shapes Reputation:

Customer connections are not isolated events; they contribute to the larger perception of a brand's reputation. Every positive interaction becomes a brushstroke that paints a favourable picture in the customer's mind.

Continuous Learning is Essential:

Customer preferences and expectations evolve. Continuous learning from customer interactions is essential for staying ahead of the curve, adapting strategies, and ensuring ongoing customer satisfaction.

Trust is Earned, Not Given:

Trust is not a given; it's earned through consistent, positive interactions. Building trust requires time, effort, and a genuine commitment to meeting and exceeding customer expectations.

The Cycle

The B2B Customer Lifecycle is an H2H (human-to-human) relationship steering journey across all its stages. It is like navigating through the waters of human relationships, where each stage owner plays a role in shaping successful partnerships.

Here is a look at the lifecycle stages.

Demand Generation to Lead: The journey commences with sparking interest and generating demand. Strategic marketing efforts and engaging content transform curious minds into potential leads, igniting paths ahead.

Lead to Order: Leads give a potential opportunity to form a valuable partnership. Through strategic nurturing, personalised engagement, and effective communication, a lead transforms into an order.

Order to Fulfilment: The order marks the birth of a promise. From the moment an order is placed, it's a race against time to ensure seamless delivery. Effective communication, streamlined processes, and efficient logistics orchestrate the magic that transforms an order into a reality.

Fulfilment to Billing: As products or services reach the hands of customers, the journey continues with transparent and accurate billing. Precise invoicing, financial clarity, and prompt communication contribute to a harmonious transition from fulfilment to billing.

Billing to Payment: From the invoice's arrival to the final payment received, this stage is about financial synergy. A smooth and hassle-free payment process enhances trust and sustains the momentum of the partnership.

Payment to Renewal: Successful partnerships transcend transactions. As the current service nears its contracted term, effective account management, value demonstration, and understanding of evolving needs pave the way for a renewal that's not just a formality but a celebration of mutual success.

Renewal to Expansion: Renewal is the foundation; expansion is the aspiration. As trust deepens, exploring ways to further support customers' growth becomes paramount. Proactive solutions, new opportunities, and tailored offerings form the cornerstone of this growth-focused phase.

Expansion to Advocacy: An empowered partnership evolves into advocacy. As customers experience value, they become ambassadors. Their positive feedback, referrals, and endorsements drive the brand's growth in the market.

Advocacy to Refinement: Even advocates seek refinement. Continuously engaging with your advocates helps fine-tune your offerings, catering to evolving industry dynamics and client needs. Feedback loops and proactive engagement ensure you're staying relevant and responsive.

Refinement to Demand Generation: Refined strategies, insights, and innovations feed into demand generation, starting the cycle afresh.

The stages are not a linear path, though, but an ongoing cycle of growth, collaboration, and achievement. They can apply to other customer segments, too.

Money

While NPS is the heartbeat of CX, Collections efficacy is the pulse of CX. B2B and B2C collection approaches vary significantly, and by recognising these nuances, one can tailor collection strategies

On a light note,

B2B Collections is the land of big deals and complex contracts. It's all about deciphering contracts thicker than a dictionary, deciphering custom pricing that is in Morse code, and remembering more legal jargon than a seasoned lawyer.

B2C Collections is like handling a hundred tiny puzzles all at once and a jigsaw marathon! With consumer protection rules as strict as a librarian at closing time, one has to follow the book. The emphasis here is on making every customer feel like a superstar, which can be a bit like getting your cat to love you unconditionally.

Collections require you to channel your inner Sherlock Holmes.

So, In B2B, you're solving the mystery of why the money isn't where it's supposed to be, while in B2C, you're figuring out how to make people pay up while still sending them home happy.

A balancing act by a tightrope walker with an itch!

But seriously

B2B Collections:

1. *Complex Agreements:* B2B transactions often come with detailed contracts, custom pricing, and agreed-upon payment terms. Collections teams must ensure adherence to these terms

2. *Relationship Focus:* Building and maintaining strong business relationships is paramount. Collection efforts require a balance between preserving relationships and recovering outstanding payments

3. *Communication:* Communication tends to be more direct and personalised. Collections teams often engage in discussions about outstanding invoices, understanding the client's situation, and finding mutually beneficial solutions

4. *Longer Payment Cycles:* B2B payments can have longer cycles due to the nature of business operations. Collection strategies must factor in longer wait times

B2C Collections:

1. *Volume Transactions:* B2C collections involve a higher volume of transactions, often smaller in size. These could be credit card payments, instalment plans, or subscription fees

2. *Regulations:* B2C collections are subject to consumer protection laws and regulations. Collections strategies must adhere to these legal frameworks

3. *Standardisation:* B2C collections often involve standardised payment methods, making the process more streamlined and consistent

4. *Emphasis on customer experience:* With individual consumers, maintaining a positive customer experience is crucial. Collections teams need to be empathetic and adaptable.

Each One

This one is on five lessons in service strategy learned from handling various B2B customer segments. From top corporates to SMEs to government clients, each segment brings unique challenges and opportunities shared below.

Personalisation Is the Key to Success.

While serving different customer segments, personalisation is paramount. By understanding these distinct requirements, one can provide customised experiences to exceed expectations.

Top corporate customers appreciate tailored solutions that cater to specific needs and objectives.

SMEs value agility, flexibility, and personalised attention that helps their businesses thrive.

Government customers prioritise compliance, transparency, and reliable service.

Motto: One size does not fit all!

Communication Styles Matter

Effective communication is crucial when handling different customer segments. Adapting communication styles to match the preferences of each segment and building strong relationships and trust along the way is key to CX.

Corporate customers value professional and concise communication backed by thorough knowledge and expertise.

SMEs appreciate friendly and approachable communication that fosters a sense of partnership.

Government clients expect clear and formal communication that adheres to protocols & regulations.

Motto: Speak their language.

Understand Their Industry and Pain Points.

To truly serve different customer segments, one must immerse oneself in their world and gain a deep understanding of their industry, challenges, and pain points.

Top corporate customers may face complex strategic issues that require innovative solutions.

SMEs often grapple with resource limitations and operational efficiency.

Government clients navigate intricate regulations and public accountability.

By empathising with the unique struggles of each segment, one can offer valuable insights and tailor services to address their specific needs.

Motto: Be their trusted adviser!

Flexibility Breeds Customer Loyalty.

Different customer segments come with varying expectations and demands. Being adaptable and flexible is key to fostering loyalty.

Top corporate customers may require customised pricing models & exclusive offers. SMEs appreciate scalability and the ability to adapt to their changing needs. Government clients often value compliance and quick response times.

By providing flexible solutions and adapting processes, one can build long-lasting relationships and become a preferred partner.

Motto: Bend without breaking!

Continuously Seek Feedback and Improvement.

Customer segments are not static entities and need to evolve. Actively seeking feedback from each segment to know their evolving requirements helps CX. Regularly evaluating performance, identifying areas for improvement, and implementing changes accordingly helps. By doing so, one demonstrates a commitment to their success.

Motto: Be a partner in their growth journey!

People Bytes

Why?

Life is too short to be stuck in a job you don't enjoy. The real secret to success and fulfilment is to love what you do. When you're passionate about your work, it doesn't feel like a job; it becomes a journey of self-discovery and growth.

Why does one choose CX: *The answer is that it can be a career that brings Thrill, Creativity, and Satisfaction in life.*

The Thrill of Resolution:

One of the most exhilarating aspects of CX is the thrill of solving issues. It's like being a detective, deciphering puzzles of customer dissatisfaction, and uncovering the missing pieces to make everything whole again. Every resolved problem is a victory, a testament to persistence and dedication.

The Joy of Satisfaction:

Seeing a satisfied human, whether a customer or a team member, is a source of immeasurable happiness. The smile on their face, the contentment in their tone - it's a reward that goes beyond measure. Knowing that your actions have made someone's day better is a feeling like no other.

The Canvas of Creativity:

CX is a canvas where creativity can flourish. Crafting exceptional experiences requires thinking outside the box, innovating, and personalising interactions. It's an opportunity to create and design moments that are not just good but unforgettable.

The Challenge of Optimisation:

One can fall in love with the challenge of making operations tighter, smoother, and better. It's like fine-tuning a well-oiled machine. The process involves constant improvement and finding ways to enhance efficiency without compromising quality, and many find this challenge both intellectually stimulating and rewarding.

The Feedback Loop:

Last but not least, the wonderful feedback that comes with CX work is invaluable. It's like a compass, guiding you to what's working and what needs adjustment. The feedback loop helps one evolve, delivering even better experiences and exceeding customer expectations.

In a world where every interaction matters, CX does offer a fulfilling career. So, if you've ever wondered why someone would choose a career in customer experience, it's because it's a world of constant discovery, satisfaction, and growth, too, just as any other.

Come on Aboard!

Let's see what leaders look for when they hire who they hire for various roles of CX. While the picture gives a broad view, here are some qualities of people best suited for CX other than the regular ones usually spoken about, such as a customer-centric mindset, communication skills, and empathy.

Problem-Solving Prowess: CX is often about turning challenges into opportunities. Those who possess strong problem-solving skills are the navigators who can steer your CX ship through turbulent waters and toward smoother seas.

Adaptability: The CX landscape is ever-changing. Candidates who embrace change and thrive in dynamic environments are your agile adventurers, ready to tackle whatever CX challenges come their way.

Attention to Detail: Sometimes, the smallest details can make the biggest impact on CX. Those who are meticulous and committed to delivering flawless experiences are the architects of CX excellence.

Team Player Mentality: CX is a collective effort. Look for candidates who can harmonise with others, collaborate seamlessly, and contribute to a positive team dynamic.

Data-Driven Insight: CX often relies on data analytics to uncover insights. Individuals who are comfortable working with data and drawing meaningful conclusions from it are the data explorers who can help you chart an improvement course.

Passion for Learning: The CX landscape is continually evolving. Seek candidates who have a thirst for knowledge and a passion for staying up-to-date with industry trends and innovations.

Resilience: CX can sometimes be challenging, especially when dealing with difficult situations. Those who exhibit resilience can weather storms and keep the CX ship sailing smoothly.

Hiring for CX isn't just about filling a role; it's about selecting individuals who will be the custodians of your brand's relationship with its customers.

Certify for Success

While good leaders sift through CX resumes, especially those of experienced professionals, one thing that impresses me is a commitment to learning through certifications. The true mark of an exceptional professional isn't just the roles they've held but their eagerness to keep learning. Experience is invaluable, but in a world that's evolving faster than you can say "innovation," a commitment to continuous learning is like having a superpower. It's that thirst for knowledge that keeps you agile, adaptable, and ready to conquer new horizons.

In the field of CX, here are some generic certifications that confirm basic learning, besides regular domain-related certifications of evolving technologies.

1. **PMP (Project Management Professional):** A PMP certification is incredibly beneficial for CX professionals. It equips you with the skills to lead and manage CX initiatives or even B2B deliveries, ensuring projects are completed efficiently and effectively.

2. **Design Thinking Certification:** Design thinking is a powerful tool for CX professionals as it fosters innovation and customer-centric solutions.

3. **ITIL (Information Technology Infrastructure Library):** Especially relevant if you're working in a technology-driven CX environment, ITIL certifications provide an understanding of IT service management and how it relates to customer-focused service delivery.

4. **CCMP (Certified Change Management Professional):** CX often involves change management, making CCMP a valuable certification. It equips you with the skills to guide teams and organisations through changes, ensuring minimal disruption to the customer experience.

5. **Lean Six Sigma Certification:** Lean Six Sigma methodologies are all about process improvement. By achieving a Green or Black Belt certification, you become proficient in identifying and resolving process inefficiencies that can enhance the customer experience.

6. **COPC (Customer Operations Performance Centre) Certification:** COPC certification focuses on performance management and improvement, which is vital for maintaining high standards in the CX centre of operations.

7. **Digital Marketing Certifications:** In the digital age, an understanding of digital marketing is essential for CX professionals. Certifications like those from HubSpot, Google, or Hootsuite can enhance your knowledge of customer engagement strategies.

But remember, these certifications are only tools to support your CX journey. They validate your expertise and equip you with skills to navigate the ever-evolving world of customer experience. Pair these certifications with practical experience, and you'll be well-prepared to deliver exceptional customer experiences. It's the synergy of learning and real-world experience that always forges a well-rounded expert.

The Mind

Entrepreneurship is a mindset that needs not be restricted to founders and business owners. Here is how you can inculcate entrepreneurship in customer account management.

Embrace a Customer-centric Approach.

Entrepreneurs understand that customers are the lifeblood of their business. Similarly, as a customer account manager, one should adopt a customer-centric approach. Dive deep into understanding their unique needs, challenges, and goals. Be their trusted adviser, providing tailored solutions and going the extra mile to exceed their expectations. By putting the customer at the centre of everything we do, we create strong and lasting partnerships.

Think Like a Problem-solver and Opportunity-seeker.

Entrepreneurs are natural problem-solvers, constantly seeking opportunities for growth and improvement. Apply this mindset to customer account management by proactively identifying pain points, addressing challenges, and presenting innovative solutions. Be on the lookout for upselling and cross-selling opportunities, helping your customers maximise their potential. By adopting an entrepreneurial lens, one can become a strategic partner, driving mutual success.

Cultivate a Growth Mindset and Stay Curious.

Entrepreneurs understand that growth comes from continuous learning and embracing new ideas. Similarly, in customer account management, cultivate a growth mindset. Stay curious about your customers' industries, trends, and emerging technologies. Attend industry events, read relevant publications, and network with thought leaders. By nurturing your knowledge, one becomes a trusted adviser who brings fresh perspectives and valuable insights to the table.

Build Meaningful Relationships and Foster Loyalty.

Entrepreneurs know that building strong relationships is the foundation of long-term success. As customer account managers, prioritise building meaningful connections with your customers. Take the time to listen, understand their goals, and provide personalised experiences. Be proactive in your communication, offer support, and show genuine care. By fostering loyalty and trust, one becomes a vital partner in one's journey, solidifying one's business relationships.

Embrace Resilience and Learn from Setbacks.

Entrepreneurs understand that setbacks are inevitable but view them as opportunities for growth. In customer account management, embrace resilience and learn from challenges. When faced with obstacles, stay calm, analyse the situation, and adapt your approach. Use setbacks as stepping stones for improvement and innovation. By showing resilience and determination, one builds a reputation as a reliable partner who can weather any storm.

So, whether you're an entrepreneur or a customer account manager, embrace the entrepreneurial mindset to elevate your account management game and become an invaluable asset to your customers!

Polka Dots

How fast can you connect the dots and solve a complex work challenge or CX issue?

The ability to connect the dots is a success factor that gets honed as you handle diverse portfolios and people. Becoming a dot connector is about seeing patterns where others see chaos, finding solutions in complexity, and creating a solution with seemingly disparate elements or departments.

Connecting the dots is, however, not just about problem-solving but seeing opportunities, predicting trends, and steering your career to what you want to do most.

Here's a guide to cultivating this:

Embrace Diverse Perspectives: Actively seek exposure to diverse perspectives within and outside your organisation. Engage with different departments and attend technology displays to broaden outlooks.

Cross-Functional Projects: If bandwidth allows, dive into cross-functional projects. Working across departments enhances your understanding of various business functions, fosters collaboration, and uncovers hidden connections.

Read Widely: Immerse yourself in the experiences and insights of successful business leaders. Reading about the challenges they faced, the strategies they employed, and the solutions they devised provides a rich source of inspiration and learning.

Continuous Learning: The corporate landscape is ever-evolving. Stay ahead by committing to continuous learning. Attend workshops, trainings, and conferences. Keep your skills sharp and your knowledge current to better connect the dots.

Curiosity As a Driving Force: Be relentlessly Curious. Ask questions, seek understanding, and challenge assumptions. A curious mindset propels you to explore beyond the obvious and discover novel connections.

Here are some limiting behaviours to build the ability to connect the dots.

Rigidity in Thinking: A rigid mindset, resistant to new ideas and perspectives, is a significant deterrent to connecting the dots.

Fear of Failure: The fear of failure can paralyse creative thinking. Connecting the dots often involves trial and error, experimentation, and the occasional misstep. Averse to failure, individuals may avoid the necessary risks for fear of being wrong.

Ego-Driven Decision Making: Decision making fuelled by ego and the desire for personal validation can cloud objectivity. Egoists might prioritise their ideas over more innovative solutions, stifling the process of connecting the dots.

Overreliance on Assumptions: Building connections requires a foundation of accurate information. Relying too heavily on assumptions without seeking data-driven insights can lead to misguided connections and flawed conclusions.

By connecting dots and understanding the ecosystem by seeing how each dot fits into the larger context, you'll discover richer, more meaningful connections and careers.

Are You There Yet?

Challenging moments in life often offer the richest opportunities for growth, especially in the realm of CX careers, which are honed by navigating stormy seas. Here are the top ten narratives that stand out as a necessary experience in CX B2B leadership.

1. The High-Stakes Service Disruption

Managing customer communications during a critical service disruption is a high-stakes challenge. Balancing transparency, reassurance, and a proactive plan of action becomes paramount as we work tirelessly to restore normalcy.

2. Unravelling Complex Technical Issues

Addressing intricate technical issues demands delicacy, clarity, and patience. Simplifying concepts for customers while assuring them of resolution requires a meticulous approach

3. Negotiating Contractual Challenges

Tackling negotiations and disputes over contractual terms present diplomatic hurdles. Maintaining a professional tone, empathising with customer concerns, and working towards fair resolutions are central to defusing tension.

4. Managing Expectations in Product Rollouts

Launching products brings excitement but also raises expectations. Effectively managing communications during rollout, addressing initial hiccups, and articulating long-term benefits require strategic messaging.

5. Handling Sensitive Complaints

Navigating through emotionally charged customers demands a delicate touch. Acknowledging grievances, expressing genuine concern, and offering solutions while maintaining composure are key elements.

6. Crisis Communication During Market Challenges

Addressing customer concerns during market challenges tests our crisis communication strategies. Maintaining brand integrity, instilling confidence, and outlining a path forward requires a blend of transparency and optimism.

7. Regulatory Compliance Issues

Grappling with customer communications around regulatory compliance poses its own set of challenges. Clearly articulating changes, ensuring understanding, and providing support during transitions are pivotal.

8. Cultural Sensitivity

Managing communications across diverse cultural landscapes requires heightened sensitivity. Adapting messages to resonate with varied audiences while avoiding missteps demands an understanding of nuanced cultural dynamics.

9. Addressing Product Recalls

Navigating the complexities of product recalls involves urgent and clear communication. Balancing the seriousness of the situation with a commitment to customer needs is a delicate tightrope walk.

10. Humanising Automated Interactions

Implementing automated systems while maintaining a human touch poses a unique challenge. Infusing warmth, empathy, and a sense of personalised attention into automated interactions requires innovative approaches.

Each of these brings lessons in resilience, adaptability, and trust essential in CX leadership because often, service leadership is much more than meets the eye.

Murphy

Are you ready to face any ball that life throws at you? In the unpredictable world of corporate life and CX, one often comes face to face with the unexpected. Deadlines shift, technology fails, and plans take unexpected turns. But fear not! There exists a trusty companion to manoeuvre these and learn from - Murphy's Law!

The Murphy's Law states, "Anything that can go wrong will go wrong." While it might sound daunting, embracing Murphy's Law can be liberating. Here's why this famous law is a steadfast companion in corporate CX adventures.

Expect the Unexpected:

Murphy's Law teaches one to anticipate and embrace the unexpected. Instead of being caught off guard when things don't go according to plan, we become prepared for any twists and turns that come our way.

Learning: Stay agile and adaptable, and turn obstacles into opportunities!

Problem-Solving Superpowers:

Murphy's Law puts problem-solving skills to the test. When things go awry, one can tap into their creativity, resilience, and resourcefulness to find innovative solutions. Each challenge becomes a chance to showcase our abilities and prove that we can overcome any hurdle.

Learning: Embrace the thrill of solving problems head-on!

Building Resilience:

Murphy's Law strengthens one's resilience muscles. We learn to bounce back from setbacks, rise above adversity, and keep moving forward. With each unexpected twist, one becomes more resilient and better equipped to handle whatever corporate life throws their way.

Learning: Rise like phoenixes, stronger than ever!

Humour and Perspective:

Murphy's Law teaches one to find humour in the chaos. Laughter is a secret weapon when things go haywire. By maintaining a sense of humour, we keep things in perspective and prevent stress from consuming us.

Learning: Laugh off the mishaps and celebrate our ability to navigate through the storm!

Learning and Growth:

Murphy's Law presents one with valuable learning opportunities. Each misstep teaches lessons that we carry with us throughout our corporate journey. We gain wisdom, refine our strategies, and become more equipped to handle future challenges.

Learning: Let's embrace the lessons, grow, and evolve as professionals!

So, welcome Murphy's Law with open arms in CX and the corporate world. It's here to remind us of our resilience, problem-solving prowess, and ability to adapt to any situation. Let's embrace the unexpected, find humour in the chaos, and conquer the CX world with determination!

Tech Tango

Here are three people's lessons gathered from the trenches of technical support. These are capabilities that one needs to find when hiring for technical support beyond qualifications and hard skills.

Capability #1: Practicing the fine art of turning jargon into plain English.

The mystical language of tech jargon is a peculiar dialect that only tech wizards truly comprehend. The true technical ace has honed their skills in the fine art of translating tech mumbo-jumbo into plain English. One must constantly remember that it's not about flaunting knowledge; it's about helping others understand the enigmatic world of technology without feeling like they've stumbled into an alien spaceship.

Capability #2: The delicate art of calming the tech rage.

In the field of technical support, one will encounter customers who are teetering on the edge of tech-induced frustration. Is the ace skill needed? The ability to transform their rage into calm, zen-like states. One needs to master the art of defusing anger with soothing words, the occasional humour, and the promise of a resolution that can leave customers with content that they are in good hands. Remember, empathy is the best antivirus against tech rage!

Capability #3: Navigating the ever-changing landscape of tech trends.

In this fast-paced digital world, staying on top of the latest tech trends is like riding a rollercoaster blindfolded. It can be time-consuming and occasionally makes tech aces want to scream at the pace. But technical aces need to embrace the constant learning, adapt like chameleons, and remember to buckle up for the occasional confusion.

Superpowers

Three life lessons in customer account management leadership with a dash of Marvel movies. As a customer account leader, a large part of your work will revolve around leading customer account management teams for sales, service, and collections. Collaboration skills help make this more effective as a leader is expected to turn the team into a performing unit.

Lesson #1:

Unleashing Your Team's Superpowers.

In any team, each member possesses unique superpowers. Some can calm even the most irate customers with soothing voices, while others have the knack for solving complex issues faster than a speeding bullet.

So, embrace the team members' superpowers and recognise the strengths of your colleagues. Together, you'll be an unstoppable force, ready to conquer challenges that come your way.

Lesson #2:

Building Bridges With the Internal Avengers.

As customer account heads, recognise that you are not alone in this endeavour. Every organisation has its own internal Avengers – the talented individuals from different departments who possess skills you or the team may lack. From the technical gurus to the billing wizards, their collaboration is essential for your success. To be honest, sometimes, understanding their jargon can feel like deciphering an alien language. However, a little smile goes a long way. Embrace the jargon, ask questions, and find common ground. Together, you can build bridges that connect, creating a dynamic force that saves the day, one customer at a time!

Lesson #3:

Harnessing the Collective Superpowers for Ultimate Customer Delight.

When you combine your superpowers and collaborate with Avengers, you can create an extraordinary customer experience that's as epic as any Marvel movie. All your unique strengths come together like Forces uniting, each contributing their expertise to deliver solutions that can leave customers amazed.

Remember to take a moment to appreciate the collaboration, laugh at the occasional mishaps, and celebrate the victories, big or small. Your customers are counting on you to save the day!

All That I Do

As industries evolve and customer expectations soar, a new transition from customer service has emerged on the CX landscape—the role of customer success. Unlike traditional customer service roles, customer success is not just about resolving issues; it's about fostering long-term relationships, driving value realisation, and ensuring the success and satisfaction of every customer. Read on to delve into the key aspects of customer success and its differentiation from traditional customer service roles across various industries:

Proactive Relationship Building

Customer Success goes beyond reactive problem-solving to proactive relationship building. Customer Success professionals actively engage with customers to understand their goals, challenges, and needs and then proactively work to anticipate and address them before they arise. This proactive approach fosters trust, loyalty, and a sense of partnership between the customer and the company.

Value Realisation and Optimisation

While customer service focuses on resolving immediate issues, customer success is all about driving value realisation and optimisation. Customer Success professionals help customers unlock the full potential of the product or service, identify opportunities for growth and improvement, and continuously align solutions with the evolving needs and objectives of the customer.

Strategic Advisory and Consultation

Customer Success professionals serve as strategic advisers and consultants, guiding customers on how to best leverage the company's offerings to achieve their desired outcomes. They provide insights, best practices, and industry knowledge to help customers overcome challenges, capitalise on opportunities, and stay ahead of the curve in their respective industries.

Data-Driven Insights and Actionable Intelligence

In the age of big data and analytics, customer success relies heavily on data-driven insights and actionable intelligence. Customer Success professionals analyse customer data, usage patterns, and feedback to identify trends, uncover opportunities, and drive continuous improvement. This data-driven approach enables proactive decision making and personalised engagement with customers.

Long-Term Relationship Management

While customer service often focuses on resolving one-off issues, customer success is all about building and nurturing long-term relationships. Customer Success professionals stay engaged with customers throughout their journey, from onboarding and implementation to adoption, renewal, and advocacy. They serve as trusted partners, advocates, and champions for the customer within the company.

So, in summation, customer success roles represent a paradigm shift in how companies engage with and serve their customers. By focusing on proactive relationship building, value realisation, strategic advisory, data-driven insights, and long-term relationship management, customer success redefines the customer experience and drives sustainable growth and success across industries.

In Your Shoes

In the intricacies of customer experience (CX), one feeling - empathy reigns supreme as the guiding force that transforms transactions into meaningful connections and customers into loyal advocates. The best customer representative is one who can empathise, which means to understand, relate to, and address the needs and emotions of customers with compassion and authenticity.

However, the question arises: Can empathy truly be cultivated in hires, or is it an innate quality that must be present from the start?

The truth, as always, is somewhere in between—a delicate balance of nature and nurture, where hiring individuals with a predisposition for empathy sets the stage for success, while intentional cultivation and reinforcement further amplify its impact.

Here's a five-pronged strategy to foster empathy in customer representatives and make it the cornerstone of your CX strategy:

Prioritise Emotional Intelligence (EI) in Hiring

"Empathy begins with understanding life from another person's perspective." - Harper Lee. When screening candidates for customer-facing roles, look beyond technical skills and qualifications. Seek individuals with high emotional intelligence, strong communication skills, and a genuine desire to connect with others.

Immersive Training and Development

"Empathy is seeing with the eyes of another, listening with the ears of another, and feeling with the heart of another." - Alfred Adler. Provide comprehensive training programmes that immerse new hires in the customer's journey, emphasising the importance of active listening, perspective-taking, and emotional resonance. Role-playing exercises, real-life scenarios, and shadowing experienced representatives can help hone empathy skills in a practical context.

Lead by Example

"The way we talk to our children becomes their inner voice." - Peggy O'Mara. Cultivate a culture of empathy from the top down, with leaders demonstrating compassionate communication and genuine concern for both customers and team members. When employees see empathy in action, they are more likely to emulate it in their interactions.

Feedback and Recognition

"Recognition is the greatest motivator." - Gerard C. Eakedale. Regularly recognise and reward acts of empathy and exceptional customer service. Provide constructive feedback and coaching to help representatives continuously refine their empathetic skills and address areas for improvement.

Empowerment and Support

"Empathy is about standing in someone else's shoes, feeling with his or her heart, seeing with his or her eyes." - Daniel H. Pink. Empower customer representatives with the autonomy and resources they need to make empathetic decisions and resolve customer issues effectively. Offer ongoing support, encouragement, and mentorship to foster a culture of empathy and resilience.

Let's embrace empathy as the cornerstone of our CX strategy and pave the way for meaningful connections, memorable experiences, and unwavering customer loyalty.

Never

"In the absence of structural improvement, transactions are merely Band-Aids on deep wounds." - Unknown.

A great service leader can transform your organisation, while a bad one can destroy it in all ways. How do you know that the person at the helm of your service leadership has the right traits? It's essential to recognise the traits that can hinder progress and ultimately lead to subpar customer experiences.

Here's a glimpse into what a bad service leader looks like:

Neglect of Employee Experience (EX)

"Customers will never love a company until the employees love it first." - Simon Sinek. These leaders fail to acknowledge that Employee Experience (EX) is intrinsically linked to customer experience (CX). Ignoring the well-being and development of employees ultimately impacts the quality of service provided to customers.

Limited Exploration of Voice of Customer (VoC)

"Your most unhappy customers are your greatest source of learning." - Bill Gates. These leaders overlook the Voice of the Customer (VoC) and do not delve into customer feedback and insights in detail. Consequently, they miss out on valuable opportunities for improvement and innovation.

Disregard for Capability or Strategy Teams

"Alone we can do so little; together we can do so much." - Helen Keller. These leaders do not believe in investing in capability teams that focus on building and refining processes. Instead, they prioritise individuals who handle transactions without considering the broader structural capabilities needed for sustainable growth.

Transactional Focus

"Too often we are so preoccupied with the destination, we forget the journey." - Unknown. A bad service leader prioritises short-term transactions over long-term structural improvements. They are content with addressing immediate issues without considering underlying systemic issues.

Overemphasis on Transaction handling individuals

"Quality is not an act; it is a habit." - Aristotle. They place more importance on individuals who handle transactions efficiently rather than recognising the value of those who contribute to building structural capabilities within the organisation.

Safety in Transactions Mentality

"Safety is not always the absence of danger, but the presence of values." - Unknown. They adopt a mindset that views more transactions as safer, equating quantity with success rather than focusing on the quality and impact of each interaction.

Lack of Brainstorming

"Innovation distinguishes between a leader and a follower." - Steve Jobs. These leaders fail to foster a culture of brainstorming and innovation within their team, stifling creativity and missing out on potential solutions to challenges.

Failure to Benchmark Competition

"The only way to do great work is to love what you do." - Steve Jobs. These leaders do not benchmark themselves against competitors or industry standards, limiting their ability to identify areas for improvement and innovation.

Servile Attitude

"The first step to leadership is servanthood." - John C. Maxwell. These leaders demonstrate a servile attitude towards customers, prioritising compliance over proactive problem-solving and relationship building.

Lack of Customer Interaction

"Your most unhappy customers are your greatest source of learning." - Bill Gates. These leaders are disconnected from customers and do not actively seek opportunities to engage with them, missing out on valuable insights and opportunities for improvement.

Inability to Connect Functional Dots

"The strength of the team is each member. The strength of each member is the team." - Phil Jackson. They struggle to connect the dots between different functions within the organisation, resulting in siloed efforts and disjointed customer experiences.

Recognising and addressing these traits is crucial for fostering a culture of excellence and delivering exceptional service to customers.

First Amongst Equals

In the ever-evolving phases of customer experience (CX), two crucial pillars stand tall: Strategy and Operations. While distinct in their focus and approach, both are indispensable components of a successful CX framework. Let's explore the differences and the invaluable role each plays:

Strategy Teams

"Strategy without tactics is the slowest route to victory; tactics without strategy is the noise before defeat." - Sun Tzu. The Strategy team is the visionary architect, charting the course for the organisation's CX journey. They analyse market trends, customer insights, and competitive landscapes to develop a roadmap that aligns with overarching business objectives. Their strategic foresight lays the foundation for innovation and differentiation in the CX realm.

Operations Teams

"The key to success is to focus on goals, not obstacles." - Unknown. In contrast, the operations team is the engine that drives the day-to-day execution of CX initiatives. They translate strategic objectives into actionable plans, ensuring seamless implementation across various touchpoints. From optimising processes to managing resources and resolving customer issues, their meticulous attention to detail keeps the CX machine running smoothly.

While Strategy and Operations may operate in different spheres, they are intrinsically linked and equally necessary for CX's success:

Alignment

"Great things in business are never done by one person. They're done by a team of people." - Steve Jobs. The Strategy team sets the vision, while the operations team ensures alignment and execution. Their collaboration ensures that every action is purposeful and contributes to overarching goals.

Adaptability

"It is not the strongest of the species that survive, nor the most intelligent, but the one most responsive to change." - Charles Darwin. Strategy provides the roadmap, but operations navigates the twists and turns of real-world implementation. Their ability to adapt and iterate ensures that CX initiatives remain relevant and effective in a rapidly changing landscape.

Customer-Centricity

"Your most unhappy customers are your greatest source of learning." - Bill Gates. Both teams share a common goal: to deliver exceptional experiences that delight customers. While Strategy teams identify opportunities for innovation, operations teams ensure that these innovations translate into tangible value for customers.

Strategy and operations teams are two sides of the same coin. While Strategy provides the vision and direction, operations bring that vision to life through meticulous execution. Together, they form a dynamic partnership that drives continuous improvement and innovation, ultimately delivering memorable experiences that set brands apart in the hearts and minds of customers.

Process Bytes

Music & Jobs

"Design is not just what it looks like and feels like. Design is how it works."

The immortal words of Steve Jobs should resound every time you oversee a new product launch or variant to define its customer journey.

Let's use the theme of music here to illustrate the importance of Service Design in Product design.

During product creation and rollouts, the absence of service design can lead to a symphony without harmony. Here are some repercussions:

Imagine a sleek, state-of-the-art gadget, beautifully designed, yet its functionality is like an intricate puzzle without instructions.

Key Notes on Service Design Absence:

User Frustration Symphony:

Without service design, users might face a perplexing journey post-purchase. From setup challenges to unaddressed issues, the experience becomes a frustrating sonata.

Operational Discord:

Service teams, lacking a designed support structure, find themselves in a constant battle to troubleshoot. The absence of predefined processes can lead to chaos and inefficiency.

Customer Dissonance:

When customers encounter problems, and there's no seamless support mechanism, dissatisfaction crescendos. The lack of a designed service experience may turn loyal customers into critics.

Here Are a Couple of Quotes to Echo the Sentiment:

"To design is to communicate clearly by whatever means you can control or master." - Milton Glaser.

"Good design is good business." - Thomas J. Watson

Picture now a scenario where not only is the product aesthetically pleasing but is also accompanied by a service design that orchestrates a smooth post-purchase journey.

Keynotes on Service Design Presence:

User Delightful Harmony:

Users are guided through setup with intuitive support. Issues are swiftly addressed, transforming frustration into delight.

Operational Rhapsody:

Service teams work in unison, following a well-designed playbook. This operational harmony reduces response times and ensures efficient issue resolution.

Customer Symphony:

Customers become advocates, singing praises not just for the product's design but for the entire experience. This positive sentiment resonates far and wide.

In Conclusion:

In the design symphony, both product and service design play crucial roles. The absence of one can lead to customer cacophony, while their harmonious integration can produce a masterpiece.

Design, when holistic, doesn't just create products; it crafts experiences that resonate.

KISS

Keep it Simple, Stupid (KISS) is an acronym that defines the best in CX and Life because simplicity is truly the ultimate sophistication.

The art of crafting an exceptional CX begins with simplicity for the employees dealing with CX.

The Tale of Two Cafés:

Once upon a latte-scented morning, in the bustling streets of Anytown, there were two cafés. Café SimpliciTea had a straightforward process - take orders, brew coffee or tea, and serve with a smile. Café ConfusiOn the other hand, there was a labyrinth of procedures, confusing menus, and frazzled staff.

Now, imagine their employees as the protagonists. At SimpliciTea, staff glided through their tasks with grace, taking time to connect with customers, making the café hum with delight. Over at Café ConfusiOn, employees were lost in their maze. They fumbled with the coffee machine's countless buttons, mixed up orders, and sighed in frustration.

The Link Between EX and CX:

The simplicity of Café SimpliciTea's processes had a profound effect on Employee Experience (EX). Their staff felt confident and capable, which translated into genuine, warm interactions with customers. It was evident in the smiles, in the smoothness of service, and in the returning patrons.

In contrast, Café ConfusiOn's chaos affected EX negatively. Overwhelmed staff couldn't engage with customers as they wished.

The mood was tense, and the flavour of frustration seeped into every cup of coffee.

Why Simple Processes Matter:

Empowerment: Simple processes empower employees. When they're not wrestling with convoluted systems, they can direct their focus toward customers, the heart of CX.

Consistency: Simple systems make it easier to maintain consistent service. Each customer knows what to expect, which builds trust.

Adaptability: Simple processes are nimble. They allow employees to adjust to unique customer needs swiftly, creating moments of surprise and delight.

Crafting Simplicity in CX:

True service leadership is about understanding employees' challenges while dealing with customers and simplifying ruthlessly.

Simplify the tools they use, Simplify the procedures they follow, and simplify the scripts they recite!

Simplicity isn't about dumbing down; it's about smartening up. It's about freeing employees to deliver exceptional CX by reducing the cognitive load. And when employees experience less chaos, customers experience more of what truly matters – genuine, memorable interactions.

In this tale of two cafés, SimpliciTea's secret ingredient was simplicity, weaving a narrative where EX painted the most vibrant strokes on CX's canvas.

So, remember, when in doubt, keep it simple, and you might just create a masterpiece.

Getting Closer

"Do the Gemba" is not a dance but a CX practice that can give great power to business heads who made it part of their reviews. *In the office, we theorise, and on the Gemba, we realise, is the root philosophy of Gemba.*

The best ideas often come from the people closest to the work because, truly, data is just a compass, but Gemba is the map. Gemba, a term derived from Japanese lean manufacturing principles, has transcended its origins to become a guiding philosophy for those seeking to truly understand and improve processes. For CX leaders, Gemba isn't just a physical place; it's a mindset, a journey into the heart of customer interactions.

Gemba is not a retrospective glance but a real-time revelation. It's about being present where the action happens, understanding the dynamics as they unfold, and gaining insights that escape the confinement of reports.

Top Gemba exercises that CX leaders should follow frequently to improve CX are

- watching and hearing a contact centre agent manoeuvre systems and answer calls while finding the right information for customers
- visiting along with a field engineer as they travel to customer premises while charting his schedule and completing repairs
- observing remote troubleshooting by technical teams
- attending training sessions for front-liners

- last but not least, watching the navigation of competition products and apps

Why Gemba for CX Leaders?

Real-Time Insights:

Gemba provides real-time, unfiltered insights into customer interactions. It's not about waiting for reports; it's about witnessing the customer journey as it unfolds.

Understanding the Frontline Challenges:

CX leaders stepping into Gemba gain a profound understanding of the challenges faced by frontline teams. This empathy becomes the foundation for strategic decisions that address the root of issues.

Cultivating a Customer-Centric Culture:

Gemba isn't just a visit; it's a mindset. CX leaders who embrace Gemba foster a culture where everyone, from leadership to frontline staff, is aligned with the pulse of customer needs.

Driving Targeted Improvements:

Gemba empowers leaders to make targeted, impactful improvements. It's not a shot in the dark; it's a precision tool honed by firsthand experience.

Aligning Strategy with Reality:

The insights gained from Gemba ensure that CX's strategies align with the reality of customer interactions. It's a compass that can guide leaders to make decisions rooted in the actual place where customer experiences unfold.

Gemba can not only uncover hidden facets of the customer journey but has the potential to also become a catalyst for positive change.

Map my World!

How do you reach a destination while travelling through unknown terrains? A GPS helps! Process mapping is the GPS that provides exceptional CX. Here's how investing in it helps and its elements:

The Big Picture: Process mapping zooms out to give you the 10,000-foot view of your CX landscape. You can identify bottlenecks, detours, and shortcuts.

Efficiency: Just like a GPS guides down the fastest route, process mapping helps streamline CX operations. It pinpoints areas where you can cut down on time, resources, or even potholes.

Teamwork: CX teams are co-pilots, and a clear flight plan (process map) to navigate helps. When everyone understands their role and how it fits into the bigger picture, CX soars.

Consistency: Imagine if your GPS gave different directions every time you entered the same destination. Frustrating? Process mapping ensures that CX remains consistent, no matter who's at the wheel.

Here are elements of a good process with some humour

Objectives: Imagine going on a treasure hunt without knowing what the treasure is. A process should have clear objectives.

Inputs and Outputs: Just like a recipe, Inputs are ingredients, and outputs are delicious dishes.

Stakeholder Identification: Every good movie has its characters. Identify the heroes and villains in your process.

Sequencing: Have you tried putting on socks before your pants? Processes need to have a logical order.

Timelines: Timing is everything. Imagine watching a thriller where the hero takes a coffee break during a car chase. Timelines keep your process thrillingly efficient.

Resources: You wouldn't build a sandcastle with a toothpick, so ensure you have the right resources for steps.

Metrics: Like the scoreboard in a sports game, In processes, metrics are cheerleaders, keeping morale high.

Roles and Responsibilities: Like a movie cast, each actor has a role to play, and you don't want the villain doing the hero's job.

Documentation: Imagine trying to solve a murder mystery without taking notes. Chaos? Detailed documentation keeps everything organised.

Flexibility: A good process is like a dance. Sometimes, you need to freestyle when the music changes. Stick to your process, but add a little leeway if needed.

Continuous Improvement: Remember, even James Bond had to upgrade his gadgets from time to time. So Keep making it better!

Think of CX as a road trip experience. Process mapping helps design a memorable journey.

Frameworks

India's best is the best due to their quality of work. Like in the fashion industry, it could be the quality of designs, fabric, and the making process.

Quality frameworks exist to ensure product quality across industries, and there are known and tested quality tools that aid CX too in its various dimensions. So, here are some snippets on various frameworks that help when you may need to create business cases to drive CX, with some humour put in to bring clarity.

PDCA (Plan-Do-Check-Act) is like the recipe for the perfect cake: First, plan the flavour you want. Then, bake it, taste it (the best part), and if it needs more frosting, act accordingly!

DMAIC (Define-Measure-Analyse-Improve-Control): Think of it as the Sherlock Holmes approach to quality. Define the mystery, measure the clues, analyse the evidence, improve your detective skills, and control the crime scene.

FMEA (Failure Modes and Effects Analysis): Imagine yourself as a fortune teller, foreseeing potential mishaps and saving the day before they happen. "I predict a service failure at 3 PM unless we reinforce the customer support!"

Kaizen: This is like the 'Eureka!' moment of quality. Small, brilliant ideas keep popping up like bubbles in a soda can. One just needs to open it gently.

Fishbone Diagram (Ishikawa): It's the service X-ray machine. Peering inside to find the fishbones (issues) causing the patient (service) to feel unwell. Who knew service could get indigestion?

SIPOC (Supplier-Input-Process-Output-Customer): Think of it as a service recipe. You've got your suppliers (ingredients), inputs, the cooking process, and the final dish delivered to your hungry customers. Bon appétit!

5S (Sort, Set in order, Shine, Standardise, Sustain): The Marie Kondo of quality management. Tidying up the service space, ensuring everything has its place, and making it shine like a diamond.

Pareto Analysis: It's like realising that 20% of your socks take up 80% of your sock drawer. Similarly, 20% of issues cause 80% of service headaches. Time to declutter!

Root Cause Analysis: Picture yourself as a service detective. You're not just solving mysteries; you're uncovering the hidden gems of service improvement. Elementary, my dear Watson!

Voice of the Customer (VOC): This tool is like having a direct line to a customer advice hotline. "Hello, customer? I understand you need faster service and extra sprinkles? Noted!"

Conceptual clarity and implementation of these tools can help improve customer service processes. One should consider getting certified in them or trained to do so.

Y the Y

The best leaders always consciously or unconsciously use the 5Y framework while dealing with a business problem. The essence of 5Y is the art of inquiry, and the most effective leaders have perfected this well.

It's like being an Albert Einstein at your workplace, just a passionately curious mind and the 5Y!

It is, though, not a complicated math problem but a simple, powerful tool to get to the root of a problem. Imagine a curious kid continuously asking, "Why?" until they annoy the grown-ups into revealing the real story. Each subsequent "why" delves deeper, helping to peel away layers of symptoms and reach the underlying issue, thus helping find the right solutions. In the field of customer service, one can use it extensively for root cause mapping or troubleshooting, as shown below.

Problem: *Customer complaints about slow website loading times.*

1. Why is the website slow? The server response time is high.
2. Why is the server response time high? The server is overloaded.
3. Why is the server overloaded? The website's hosting plan does not accommodate peak traffic.
4. Why is the hosting plan not suitable? The initial plan was chosen without considering growth projections.
5. Why were growth projections not considered? The team lacked historical data for accurate predictions.

The 5Y or five Whys technique transcends industries. While in telecom, it uncovers the causes behind service delays. In manufacturing, it addresses quality issues. In project management, it identifies missed deadlines. The beauty lies in its universality.

Here are examples across industries

Automotive:

Problem: *Frequent breakdowns in a fleet of delivery trucks, leading to low reliability and low demand*

1. Why do the trucks break down often? Engine overheating.
2. Why does the engine overheat? Coolant levels are dropping.
3. Why are coolant levels dropping? Coolant leak due to worn-out hose.
4. Why are hoses worn-out? Hoses are not replaced during regular maintenance.
5. Why not replace during maintenance? No comprehensive checklist for maintenance.

Solution: Implement a thorough maintenance checklist that includes checking and replacing worn-out parts during regular maintenance intervals.

Healthcare:

Problem: *Long patient wait times in a medical clinic, leading to dropouts and thus lower income*

1. Why are wait times long? Limited number of doctors available.
2. Why limited doctors? High patient influx during peak hours.
3. Why a high influx? No appointment scheduling system.
4. Why is there no scheduling system? Lack of resources for implementation.
5. Why lack of resources? Budget constraints for technology investment.

Solution: Invest in an appointment scheduling system that optimises doctor availability and patient flow.

Remember, curiosity killed the cat; hence, personal advice too here is to avoid using it in friendships and Bollywood movies.

The Ruler

Five lessons on how Design Thinking helps customer service Operations & Strategy.

Mastering Design Thinking has the potential to make you a ruler of products and experiences over any other.

Lesson #1:

Empathising With Customers

Design thinking starts with empathy—the ability to understand and share the feelings of others. As customer service managers, it's crucial to put yourself in your customers' shoes. Take the time to truly understand their needs, pain points, and desires. By empathising with your customers, you can design service experiences tailored to their specific requirements. Empathy is the secret ingredient to fostering deep and meaningful connections.

Lesson #2:

Embrace a Human-centred Persona-driven Approach

Design thinking revolves around putting humans at the centre of the problem-solving process. In customer service management, embrace a human-centred approach by considering the holistic customer journey. Look beyond individual touchpoints and consider the end-to-end experience. By focusing on the human aspect, you can identify areas for improvement and create seamless, consistent, and delightful experiences at every stage. Think of customers as unique individuals, and design service solutions that cater to their needs.

Lesson #3:

Encourage a Culture of Creativity and Innovation

Design thinking thrives on creativity and innovation. One must foster a culture encouraging the customer service team to think outside the box, challenge assumptions, and generate fresh ideas. Create spaces for brainstorming and collaboration where diverse perspectives can come together to drive innovation. By embracing creativity, one can uncover new ways to solve customer problems, enhance processes, and deliver wow-worthy service experiences. Let the imagination run wild!

Lesson #4:

Prototype and Iterate for Continuous Improvement

Design thinking is an iterative process. Encourage customer service teams to prototype and test their ideas before implementing them on a larger scale. By gathering feedback and learning from real-world experiences, one can refine service strategies, identify areas of improvement, and continuously evolve your approach. Remember, iteration is the key to staying ahead of the curve and meeting ever-changing customer expectations. Embrace the journey of improvement!

Lesson #5:

Collaborate Across Departments for Holistic Solutions

In customer service management, collaboration is vital. Break down silos and collaborate with teams from different departments, such as marketing, product development, and operations. By working together, you can gain diverse insights, align goals, and design holistic solutions that address customer needs from multiple angles. Cross-functional collaboration ensures that your service strategies are aligned with the broader organisational objectives.

Maths!

At the racecourses, you learn that there is Maths to winning!
Also, in CX, knowing the principles of regression, a statistical modelling technique of Maths, helps.

In the multi-faceted landscape of customer satisfaction, identifying the key drivers of dissatisfaction is an imperative task. Imagine a scenario where there are ten contributing factors causing dissatisfaction—enter regression analysis, the compass that can guide you through this complex terrain in prioritising.

Regression analysis allows organisations to discern the weights of importance among these contributing factors. Let's consider a case where a service-oriented business faces challenges in customer satisfaction. Regression analysis unveils that responsiveness, product quality, and pricing significantly contribute to dissatisfaction. What sets regression analysis apart is its ability to move beyond a mere enumeration of factors; it assigns importance to each, offering a nuanced understanding of their impact.

For instance, a retail giant grappling with various elements affecting customer satisfaction—inventory management, checkout efficiency, and staff courtesy—can leverage regression analysis to unveil which factors weigh more heavily on dissatisfaction.

This analytical powerhouse allows organisations to prioritise and address the factors with the most significant impact, providing a roadmap for strategic interventions. It's akin to shining a spotlight on the critical elements in a sea of variables, ensuring that efforts are directed where they matter most.

In a market where customer preferences and expectations evolve swiftly, the ability to adapt is paramount. Regression analysis empowers businesses to stay agile. By understanding the importance of each dissatisfying factor, organisations can pivot quickly to address the most impactful issues, demonstrating a commitment to continuous improvement.

In conclusion, regression analysis is not just a statistical tool; it's a strategic ally in the pursuit of enhanced customer satisfaction. By unravelling the intricacies of dissatisfaction and assigning weights to contributing factors, organisations can navigate the path to improvement with precision. So, In the quest for excellence in CX, let regression analysis be a guide, illuminating the way forward.

What They Said & What They Meant!

In the fast-paced world of customer experience (CX), there is a set of jargon that will always remain constant. Read on to demystify some of the most common CX jargon, empowering you to speak the language of customer-centricity with confidence:

Customer Experience (CX)

Definition: CX encompasses all interactions and touchpoints a customer has with a company throughout their journey, from initial awareness to post-purchase support. It focuses on the overall perception and satisfaction of the customer with the brand.

Customer Journey

Definition: The customer journey maps out the various stages and touchpoints a customer goes through when interacting with a brand, from awareness and consideration to purchase and advocacy. It helps businesses understand and optimise the customer experience at each stage.

Omnichannel Experience

Definition: Omnichannel experience refers to providing a seamless and integrated experience across multiple channels and touchpoints, such as online, mobile, social media, and physical stores. It ensures consistency and continuity in the customer journey, regardless of the channel used.

Customer Touchpoints

Definition: Customer touchpoints are specific interactions or points of contact between a customer and a brand, such as website visits, social media interactions, email communications, phone calls, and in-store experiences. Optimising touchpoints is crucial for delivering a cohesive and personalised customer experience.

Net Promoter Score (NPS)

Definition: NPS is a metric used to measure customer loyalty and satisfaction by asking customers a single question: "How likely are you to recommend our product/service to a friend or colleague?" Responses are scored on a scale of 0 to 10, with promoters (scores 9-10), passives (scores 7-8), and detractors (scores 0-6) categorised accordingly.

Customer Satisfaction (CSAT)

Definition: CSAT is a metric used to measure customer satisfaction with a product or service by asking customers to rate their satisfaction on a scale (e.g., 1-5 or 1-10). It provides insights into specific interactions or experiences and helps identify areas for improvement.

Voice of Customer (VoC)

Definition: VoC refers to capturing and analysing feedback, opinions, and preferences directly from customers. It includes methods such as surveys, interviews, social media monitoring, and feedback forms to gain insights into customer needs and expectations.

Customer Persona

Definition: A customer persona is a fictional representation of a target customer segment based on demographic, psychographic, and behavioural characteristics. It helps businesses understand their customers' needs, motivations, and pain points, enabling more personalised and effective marketing and CX strategies.

Customer Empathy

Definition: Customer empathy is the ability to understand and share customers' feelings, perspectives, and experiences. It involves putting oneself in the customer's shoes, listening actively, and responding with compassion and understanding to create meaningful connections and experiences.

Customer-Centric Culture

Definition: A customer-centric culture is an organisational mindset and approach that prioritises the needs, preferences, and satisfaction of customers above all else. It involves aligning internal processes, policies, and behaviours to deliver exceptional customer experiences at every touchpoint.

Armed with this vocabulary and understanding of common CX jargon, you're ready to navigate the world of customer-centricity with clarity and confidence.

The key to success lies in putting the customer at the heart of everything you do and continuously striving to enhance their experience at every opportunity!

Keep the Money Rolling

In the competitive landscape of business, where customer expectations are continually evolving, the role of customer experience (CX) has emerged as a driving force behind revenue growth and organisational success. From attracting new customers to retaining loyal advocates, every aspect of the customer journey plays a pivotal role in shaping the bottom line. Read on to know how CX can contribute to revenue growth in an organisation:

Customer Acquisition and Retention

"Satisfied customers are the best advertisement." - Unknown. Exceptional CX attracts new customers and fosters loyalty among existing ones. By delivering personalised, seamless experiences that exceed expectations, businesses can differentiate themselves in the market, drive customer acquisition, and increase customer retention rates. Happy customers are more likely to become repeat buyers and brand advocates, contributing to long-term revenue growth.

Increased Customer Lifetime Value (CLV)

"Loyalty is not about the size of the discount. It's about the value of the relationship." - Unknown. Investing in CX initiatives that enhance customer satisfaction and engagement can lead to increased CLV. By nurturing long-term relationships, upselling/cross-selling relevant products or services, and reducing churn rates, businesses can maximise the lifetime value of each customer, resulting in sustainable revenue growth over time.

Positive Word-of-Mouth and Referrals

"Your brand is what people say about you when you're not in the room." - Jeff Bezos. Exceptional CX inspires positive word-of-mouth and referrals, amplifying brand awareness and driving organic growth. Satisfied customers are more likely to share their positive experiences with others, both online and offline, leading to increased brand visibility, credibility, and, ultimately, revenue generation through new customer acquisitions.

Brand Differentiation and Competitive Advantage

"In the age of the customer, the only sustainable competitive advantage is knowledge of and engagement with customers." - Forrester Research. In today's crowded marketplace, CX serves as a key differentiator and competitive advantage. Businesses that prioritise CX and consistently deliver memorable experiences stand out from the competition, capturing market share and driving revenue growth by attracting and retaining loyal customers.

Reduced Cost of Customer Acquisition (CAC) and Support

"It is easier to sell to satisfied customers than to acquire new ones." - Unknown. Investing in CX initiatives not only drives revenue growth but also reduces the cost of customer acquisition and support. Satisfied customers are more likely to make repeat purchases, require less support, and are more receptive to upselling/cross-selling efforts, resulting in lower CAC and support costs over time.

In conclusion, customer experience is not just a cost centre—it's a revenue driver. By prioritising CX initiatives that focus on customer satisfaction, engagement, loyalty, and advocacy, organisations can unlock sustainable revenue growth, build brand equity, and thrive in an increasingly customer-centric marketplace.

In and Out

In the crafting of customer experience (CX), a key part - contact centres serve as the frontline ambassadors of brands, bridging the gap between businesses and customers across various channels. Effective contact centre management entails striking the right balance between inbound and outbound channels, catering to diverse customer needs and preferences.

Inbound Channels

"Listening is the most powerful tool in communication." - Unknown. Inbound channels, such as phone calls, emails, and live chat, are avenues through which customers reach out to businesses for assistance, queries, or support. The focus in inbound contact centre management should be on responsiveness, empathy, and resolution. By promptly addressing customer inquiries and concerns, businesses can nurture trust and loyalty while delivering exceptional experiences.

Outbound Channels

"Proactive engagement breeds loyalty." - Unknown. Outbound channels, including proactive calls, SMS, and email campaigns, enable businesses to initiate contact with customers for various purposes, such as sales, marketing, or surveys. The focus in outbound contact centre management should be on personalisation, relevance, and value addition. By engaging customers proactively with tailored offerings or feedback requests, businesses can drive conversions, gather insights, and strengthen relationships.

The balance between inbound and outbound channels may vary depending on the specific needs and objectives of the business:

Customer Support: Inbound channels take precedence, ensuring timely and effective resolution of customer issues or inquiries. However, proactive outreach through outbound channels may be employed to preemptively address common pain points or provide updates on service disruptions.

Sales and Marketing: Outbound channels play a more prominent role, with proactive calls, emails, or SMS campaigns aimed at generating leads, nurturing prospects, and driving conversions. Inbound channels remain available to handle inquiries or provide assistance throughout the customer journey.

Feedback and Surveys: A combination of inbound and outbound channels is utilised to gather customer feedback and insights. Inbound channels facilitate real-time feedback collection during interactions, while outbound channels are leveraged for post-interaction surveys or targeted feedback campaigns.

By understanding the unique needs and preferences of your customers and leveraging both inbound and outbound channels strategically, a business can foster meaningful connections, drive engagement, and deliver exceptional experiences across the customer journey.

The Basics

In every customer experience (CX) management, transaction handling serves as a cornerstone, shaping the perceptions and loyalty of customers. To effectively gauge and improve this vital aspect of CX, we must focus on three fundamental metrics:

Transaction Count

"What gets measured gets managed." - Peter Drucker. The first step in understanding transaction handling is to quantify the volume of transactions. Tracking transaction counts provides valuable insights into customer demand, peak periods, and resource allocation needs. By monitoring transaction count, we gain a holistic view of operational efficiency and customer engagement levels.

Speed to Resolve the Transaction

"Time is of the essence." - Unknown. In today's fast-paced world, customers expect prompt and efficient resolution of their transactions. Monitoring speed to resolve transactions measures the time taken from initiation to completion, highlighting areas for process optimisation and resource allocation. A swift resolution not only enhances customer satisfaction but also reduces friction in the customer journey.

Quality of Transaction

"Quality is not an act, it is a habit." - Aristotle. Beyond quantity and speed, the quality of each transaction holds paramount importance. This metric encompasses accuracy, completeness, and adherence to service standards. By evaluating the quality of transactions, we ensure consistency and reliability, fostering trust and loyalty among customers.

Additionally, monitoring repeat transactions provides valuable insights into customer behaviour and satisfaction levels. A high volume of repeat transactions may indicate loyalty and satisfaction, while a significant number of one-time transactions may signal dissatisfaction or missed opportunities for retention.

While these internal metrics form the foundation of CX measurement in transaction handling, external measurements such as customer satisfaction scores, cost analysis, and Voice of Customer (VoC) analysis complement and enrich our understanding. By integrating both internal and external measurements, we create a comprehensive framework for continuous improvement and innovation in CX.

By mastering the fundamentals of CX measurement in transaction handling, we pave the way for enhanced operational efficiency, customer satisfaction, and long-term success.

Technology Bytes

1. *Perfect Shots*
2. *Batman & Robin*
3. *Dreams*
4. *Everywhere*
5. *Shades of Service*
6. *C U Soon*

Perfect Shots

The perfect shot in CX today lies in choosing whether one should lean into the seamless allure of self-help digital experiences or bask in the warmth of a human experience. Here is a quick take on decoding the dilemma of Digital Experience vs. Human Touch in customer interactions. This perennial debate is more than just a choice; it's a fundamental consideration that can shape the soul of customer relationships based on technological evolution.

Digital Experience: Precision and Efficiency

The allure of digital experience lies in its precision and efficiency. Automated processes, algorithms, and data analytics compose a seamless tune where transactions are swift, information is at the fingertips, and personalisation is a code away. The digital landscape promises scalability, cost efficiencies, and consistency, creating a realm where businesses can navigate with speed and accuracy.

Human Touch: Emotion and Empathy

On the other side of the spectrum, the human touch adds a different hue to the canvas of customer interactions. It's about empathy, understanding, and the art of genuine connection. Human touch goes beyond transactions; it's about forging relationships, understanding unique needs, and providing a personalised experience. It's the realm where emotions, nuances, and individuality reign supreme, which a no-touch digital experience cannot surpass.

Striking the Balance: Designing a Holistic Experience

The true balance might not lie in choosing one over the other but in designing a harmony between the digital and the human. Businesses can leverage the precision of digital tools while preserving the authenticity of human interactions. Maybe even make the human touch a differentiator based on preferences or use technology to craft the human touch better.

Tailoring Experiences to Preferences

The answer to the digital vs. human touch dilemma could rest on the unique needs and preferences of the audience. Some may prefer the swift, efficient nature of digital interactions, while others may seek the depth and personalisation that human touch brings, which, again, technologies like AI could enhance. The power lies in offering a choice and tailoring experiences to cater to diverse expectations.

The future of great customer experiences might well be a hybrid landscape where the digital and the human seamlessly coexist with their synergies that resonate with each unique customer, but it is not where one replaces the other.

Batman & Robin

CX and CRM are as interlinked as Batman and Robin in customer success, with one swooping in to save the day and the other keeping everything impeccably organised. Embarking on a CRM design journey is like finding the perfect dance partner for your business – just fewer tango lessons and more data waltzing.

Workflow Design plays an important role and mastering Workflow Management in CRM helps effective Customer Issue Analysis - so here are some rules from learnings to consider during your trysts with CRM design.

1. *Rule of Automation:*

Automating routine tasks into CRM workflows helps streamline processes, allowing CX teams to focus on complex customer issues and meaningful interactions.

2. *Rule of Integration:*

Ensuring seamless integration of CRM workflows with various customer touchpoints and communication channels provides a unified view of customer interactions for comprehensive issue analysis.

3. *Rule of Prioritisation:*

Prioritisation rules within CRM workflows help identify and address high-priority customer issues promptly, demonstrating a proactive approach to problem resolution.

4. Rule of Collaboration:

Leveraging collaborative features in CRM workflows helps enhance communication among cross-functional teams, fostering a collaborative environment for swift issue analysis and resolution.

5. Rule of Data Accessibility:

Workflows that facilitate easy access to relevant customer data empower CX professionals with insights needed for thorough issue analysis and personalised customer interactions.

6. Rule of Feedback Loop:

Integrating feedback loops into CRM workflows to capture insights from customer interactions, enabling continuous improvement and iterative refinement of issue analysis strategies.

7. Rule of Escalation:

Establishing clear escalation paths within CRM workflows for complex issues to higher tiers ensures a timely and effective resolution while maintaining transparency.

8. Rule of Documentation:

Incorporating documentation protocols within CRM workflows to capture and store information related to customer issues and create a knowledge base for future reference and analysis.

9. Rule of Proactive Monitoring:

Implementing proactive monitoring mechanisms in CRM workflows helps identify potential issues before they escalate, enabling Pre-emptive actions and maintaining a proactive approach to customer service.

10. *Rule of Reporting and Analytics:*

Integrating robust reporting and analytics tools into CRM workflows helps track key performance indicators, measure the effectiveness of issue analysis strategies, and drive data-driven decision making.

11. *Rule of Personalisation:*

Leveraging CRM workflows to incorporate personalisation elements in issue analysis and tailoring responses based on individual customer profiles and preferences helps achieve more personalised and effective resolutions.

Dreams

In the libraries of modern business, the synergy between CX and Customer Relationship Management (CRM) is akin to a well-choreographed dance, with each step contributing to customer satisfaction.

Let me share a story to illustrate this.

Imagine a bustling coffee shop where customers weave through the aroma of freshly ground beans. Our protagonist, Sanjay, a regular patron, steps in, expecting the usual seamless experience. Unbeknownst to him, the barista is armed not just with a coffee pot but also with a powerful CRM

1. Personalisation Beyond the Usual:

The barista recognises Sanjay instantly. The system seamlessly integrates data on Sanjay's preferences, noting the penchant for a dash of cinnamon in the latte. With this insight, the barista greets Sanjay with a smile, already preparing the personalised cup of perfection.

2. Effortless Communication:

As Sanjay waits, engrossed in the ambiance, a notification pops up on the barista's screen. This is a reminder that Sanjay recently provided positive feedback on the new pastry. Seizing the opportunity, the barista engages Sanjay in conversation, suggesting the freshly baked almond croissant – a delightful surprise that aligns seamlessly with Sanjay's tastes.

3. Proactive Issue Resolution:

Today, the coffee machine stutters, threatening to disrupt the flow of customer satisfaction. However, the CRM has already flagged this hiccup, and a tech support ticket is swiftly initiated. Sanjay witnessed not a glitch but a seamless transition to a backup machine; the issue was resolved before it could taint the experience.

4. Anticipating Future Desires:

Recognising that Sanjay tends to linger overwork in the cosy corner, the CRM triggers a notification for the barista to offer a complimentary refill. This proactive gesture not only delights Sanjay but showcases the establishment's commitment to understanding and fulfilling customer needs.

5. Security in Every Sip:

Sanjay's trust in this coffee shop isn't just about the beverages; it extends to the safeguarding of personal information. The CRM system, fortified with robust security measures, ensures that Sanjay's data is handled with the utmost care, fostering a relationship built on transparency and trust.

This narrative is more than just a story; it's a testament to the interdependent relationship between CX and a CRM. A good CRM doesn't just manage data; it transforms it into actionable insights that elevate customer experiences. The coffee shop, with its CRM, transforms routine transactions into memorable interactions, showcasing that in the contemporary business landscape, CX is only as good as the CRM that supports it.

Everywhere

The most common frustrating CX nowadays is narrating an issue to a chatbot, only to repeat it to a human agent and then endure the saga once more with tech support. We've all been there – the loop of disjointed customer service.

Crafting a seamless, interconnected journey across various channels—online, in-store, social media, and beyond—is undeniably challenging. That is what we call an omnichannel strategy, which is rooted in the ability to create an experience without borders.

The Complexity of Omnichannel Crafting

Imagine orchestrating a symphony where every instrument represents a different customer touchpoint. The website, the mobile app, the physical store, social media. The challenge lies not just in making each channel proficient, but in harmonising them to create a cohesive and synchronised experience.

A brand isn't just what you say, it's the omnichannel story you craft across every customer touchpoint.

An Omnichannel Odyssey: A Customer's Tale

Meet my protagonist, Sanjay, again, an online shopper in search of the perfect pair of running shoes. He navigates the brand's website, exploring various options. However, a dilemma arises – which size would be a fit?

Sanjay could send an email, then perhaps browse through a confusing chatbot interface, only to end up on a call with customer service, narrating the same story repeatedly. But not in the realm of Omnichannel CX.

In this modern saga, Sanjay encounters a chatbot on the website. After an interaction, realising the need for human assistance, the chatbot seamlessly transitions the conversation to a live chat with a customer service rep. No need for Sanjay to rehash the entire inquiry, and the agent is armed with the chatbot's insights.

The agent recommends a few suitable options. Sanjay, still uncertain, decides to take a break and resume the quest later. Enter the omnichannel magic – Sanjay receives a personalised email summarising the chat and offering a discount on the selected running shoes. The journey continues, but now it's a connected experience.

Days later, Sanjay decides to visit the physical store to try on the shoes. The attentive store associate, informed through the omnichannel system, is already aware of the preferred shoe choice. Sanjay is amazed – the online exploration seamlessly integrates with the in-store experience.

Finally, Sanjay purchased the perfect pair with the discount that was offered online. The order confirmation doesn't just arrive in the email; it's also accessible on the brand's app.

What Does This Tale Teach Us?

It's about more than just providing multiple channels for customer interaction. Omnichannel CX is the symphony orchestrating a seamless and unified experience.

For customers, the omnichannel approach meant no frustrating repetitions and no disjointed experiences.

Shades of Service

The Shades of Customer Support: Reactive, Proactive, Predictive, and Pre-emptive with technology tool enablers for reference.

Reactive Support

- Technology: The trusty 'Help Desk' software.
- Scenario: Customer rings the support hotline because, alas, the printer devoured their important document.

Reactive support is like your emergency pizza delivery hotline. You call when the craving hits, but it doesn't prevent the pizza from being eaten in the first place. It's reliable but a bit late in the game.

Proactive Support

- Technology: CRM systems with automated triggers.
- Scenario: You receive an email suggesting a password change because the system noticed some fishy login attempts.

Proactive support is like your mom reminding you to wear a jacket when it's cold outside. It anticipates your needs and offers helpful suggestions before you even realise you need them.

Predictive Support

- Technology: AI and Machine Learning algorithms.
- Scenario: Your favourite e-commerce site recommends products you didn't know you wanted but can't resist.

Predictive support is like that friend who knows your taste so well they pick out gifts you love every time. It predicts your preferences based on past behaviour, making your life easier and your wallet lighter.

Pre-emptive Support

-   Technology: Supercharged AI and data analytics.
-   Scenario: Before you even notice a glitch in your smartphone, it's fixed remotely.

Pre-emptive support is like having a guardian angel for your gadgets. It detects and solves issues before you even know they exist, leaving you wondering if your devices are psychic.

Think of these shades when you want to soar your customer service to the next level.

C U Soon

As digital landscapes evolve, the synergy between CX and UX becomes the heartbeat of user-centric design. User experience and customer experience are two sides of the same, so here are examples of how the convergence of CX and UX crafts digital harmony, resonating with every click, scroll, and interaction.

Adaptive Customisation:

In a low-speed internet scenario, a user's behaviour may shift towards prioritising text-based content over images. Platforms like Instagram and Facebook adjust by initially loading compressed or lower-resolution images, ensuring a faster and more accessible user experience in situations with limited bandwidth. Platforms like YouTube and Netflix allow users to customise video autoplay settings. In low bandwidth situations, users may choose to disable autoplay to prevent buffering delays, reflecting a shift in behaviour based on connectivity constraints.

Offline Interaction:

The behaviour of users changes when they are offline. Messaging apps like WhatsApp recognise this shift and allow users to compose messages even without an internet connection. Platforms like Kindle or Pocket offer offline reading modes, allowing users to download articles or books for later consumption, recognising the need for adaptability and continuous access.

Responsive Design for Varying Screen Sizes:

User behaviour varies across devices with different screen sizes. Responsive design principles are employed by websites and applications to ensure a seamless experience, adapting layouts and functionalities based on whether users are accessing content from a desktop, tablet, or mobile device.

Voice & Location Based Features:

In situations where users cannot easily type, such as when driving or multitasking, voice-based interactions help. Platforms like Google Search and Alexa tailor responses to accommodate voice commands. Navigation apps like Google Maps adjust interfaces when users are in a moving vehicle, simplifying interactions for a safer, user-friendly experience.

Push Notifications Preferences:

Users' tolerance for push notifications varies based on circumstances. Travel apps may send more frequent notifications when users are at an airport, providing real-time updates. However, in a meeting or during the night, users might prefer fewer interruptions, showcasing a shift in behaviour to be met.

Time-of-Day Engagement:

Users engage with social media platforms differently depending on the time of day. Platforms like Twitter may adjust content visibility algorithms to showcase relevant tweets during peak hours, recognising evolving behaviour patterns throughout the day.

Understanding how user needs evolve in various circumstances is pivotal in crafting intuitive experiences. The knowledge enables CX teams to create experiences that align with preferences and contextual challenges.

Decision Guides

1. *What not to do*
2. *Power*
3. *WIIFM*

What Not to Do

Prioritising our nation is an emotion that comes naturally. However, in life and CX - Prioritising is also the art of choosing what not to do so you can focus on what truly matters. In the corporate world of decision making needs, Prioritising is like juggling flaming torches – it's about not getting burned while impressing the audience. So, when faced with a plethora of innovative service ideas to implement and limited bandwidth, you can use the below to aid the decision making process in prioritising.

Customer Impact:

Prioritise ideas that directly address customer needs or pain points, ensuring your innovations align with enhancing the customer experience.

Strategic Alignment:

Align service innovations with your overall business strategy to ensure they contribute to organisational goals and long-term vision.

Feasibility:

Consider the practicality and feasibility of implementing each idea within your existing resources, infrastructure, and timeline.

Market Demand:

Evaluate the market demand for potential innovations, focusing on solutions that align with current trends or emerging needs.

Competitive Landscape:

Assess how each innovation positions your services relative to competitors, aiming for differentiators that set you apart in the market.

Resource Investment:

Evaluate the resource requirements, including time, budget, and manpower, associated with each service innovation idea.

Technology Integration:

Consider the compatibility of each idea with existing technologies and assess the potential for leveraging new technologies to enhance service delivery.

Scalability:

Prioritise innovations that can scale effectively as your business grows, ensuring they remain sustainable in the long run.

Employee Impact:

Evaluate how each innovation might impact your team, considering training needs, workload, and any changes to roles or processes.

Measurable Outcomes:

Clearly define metrics and KPIs to measure the success of each service innovation, ensuring a means to assess its impact and effectiveness.

Prioritising is acknowledging the finite nature of time and the infinite possibilities within it as choices become the architects of our achievements.

Power

In the realms of school, life, work, and CX, words hold power, but when words are fortified with data, they become a force to reckon with. Whether it's presenting an argument in class, navigating life's decisions, or contributing to the workplace dialogue, the importance of substantiating statements with data cannot be overstated. It's about the compelling evidence that can accompany your words.

Customer Experience (CX) is a fascinating realm, and here are ten facts backed by data that highlight the ever-evolving nature of CX:

1. Subconscious Decision Making: Research indicates that up to 95% of customer decisions are made subconsciously, emphasising the critical role of emotions and psychology in CX. (Harvard Business Review)
2. Social Media's Impact: Approximately 67% of consumers have used a company's social media site for servicing needs. Social media isn't just for marketing; it's an integral part of customer service. (J.D. Power)
3. The Power of Word-of-Mouth: A happy customer shares their experience with at least nine other people, while an unhappy one shares it with as many as sixteen people. Customer feedback is amplified in the age of social media. (American Express)
4. The Impact of Personalisation: Around 80% of consumers are more likely to purchase from brands that offer personalised experiences. Personalisation isn't a mere trend; it's a CX necessity. (Epsilon)

5. Customers Expect Instant Responses: Over 60% of consumers expect brands to respond to their queries within an hour on social media. Prompt response times are paramount in modern CX. [(The Social Habit)]

6. The Influence of Reviews: A single negative online review can cost a business about 30 customers. Positive reviews are essential, but addressing negative ones is equally vital. (Conversocial)

7. Omnichannel is Key: Brands with robust omnichannel customer engagement strategies can retain nearly 90% of their customers. Seamless interactions across multiple channels are now the standard. (Aberdeen Group)

8. AI is Rising: By 2027, it's anticipated that AI will automate 50% of customer service queries. Artificial Intelligence is rapidly becoming a driving force in CX. (Gartner)

9. The Upside of Complaints: Surprisingly, customers with resolved complaints often become more loyal than those who never had an issue. Service recovery can significantly strengthen customer loyalty. (Strativity)

10. Mobile Dominance: A staggering 52% of web traffic worldwide comes from mobile devices. Mobile-first strategies are no longer optional; they're imperative for businesses. (Statista)

These facts underscore the dynamic and multi-faceted nature of CX. To excel in this ever-changing landscape, businesses must stay informed about these trends and insights. After all, in CX, knowledge is power.

WIIFM

The most important tool in life, besides a sense of humour, is the ability to create a compelling WIIFM message. It's a simple yet profound concept that acknowledges the human desire to understand the personal benefits and relevance of any given situation or proposal.

By embracing WIIFM, you can empower yourselves to craft compelling messages, foster engagement, and create mutually beneficial relationships.

In Business and Marketing: For businesses, understanding WIIFM is the key to reaching customers effectively. By highlighting the unique value and benefits of products or services, businesses resonate with their target audience, inspiring them to act and make informed decisions.

In Leadership and Communication: Leaders who adopt the WIIFM principle connect with their teams on a deeper level. By articulating how individual efforts contribute to the team's success and align with personal goals, leaders foster motivation and commitment within their workforce.

In Personal Relationships: In our personal lives, applying WIIFM strengthens our connections with others. When we actively listen to their needs, empathise with their perspectives, and acknowledge their aspirations, we cultivate meaningful relationships built on mutual understanding.

In Negotiation and Collaboration: WIIFM is a powerful tool in negotiations, where understanding the motivations and priorities of each party leads to win-win outcomes. By recognising and addressing individual interests, collaborative solutions emerge more organically.

WIIFM stands for "What's In It For Me"

Closing Remarks

1. All of You
2. Acknowledgements

All of You

As this book ends and it's time for closing remarks, I can't help but thank the wonderful customers that I have met in my career. I have tried to classify them here as in the drudge sometimes of daily transactions; they have transcended the ordinary, leaving an indelible mark in my memory. They were not just transactions; they were stories, faces, and moments etched in memory.

The Appreciative Advocate:

There's the customer who doesn't just express satisfaction but becomes a vocal advocate. Their appreciative words resonate long after the interaction, a reminder that genuine appreciation is a two-way street.

The Challenger:

Then, there's the customer who challenges the status quo. Their inquiries aren't just questions; they are catalysts for growth. I remember the challenges they posed and the solutions we crafted together.

The Gracious Understander:

In the realm of unforeseen hiccups, there's the customer who exemplifies grace under pressure. Their understanding demeanour turns a potential hiccup into a collaborative problem-solving venture.

The Feedback Artisan:

Feedback is an art, and some customers masterfully provide constructive insights. Their words are not just commentary; they are blueprints for improvement, guiding the path toward excellence.

The Lifelong Learner:

Among the customers, there's the perpetual learner. Their curiosity sparks engaging conversations, turning routine transactions into opportunities for shared growth and knowledge exchange.

The Storyteller:

Some customers don't just share feedback; they share stories. These narratives become the threads weaving a rich tapestry of shared experiences, making the professional journey not just transactional but storytelling.

The Transformative Collaborator:

Collaborative customers are like co-pilots on the journey toward mutual success. I remember those who collaborated, shared insights, and collectively crafted solutions that transcended expectations.

The Genuine Connector:

Finally, some customers don't just seek a service or a product; they seek a connection. I remember those who valued the human aspect of interactions, forging a connection that transformed routine transactions into meaningful exchanges.

As I close with the above, I must say that each has contributed a unique brushstroke to the canvas of this book. They are more than visiting cards or names in a database; individuals who, in their own way, have shaped my understanding of customer interactions. In the run of commerce, they have added colour, depth, and also a touch of humanity to my life.

You know who you are, so thank you!! May your tribe prosper!

Acknowledgements

To my partner Joseph, for being everything and whose unwavering partnership is the foundation pillar of my journey.

To my parents for instilling in me a deep appreciation for the beauty of language and the power of words to inspire and connect in various ways.

To all those I've had the privilege of interacting with throughout my professional journey, both at work and within the industry, whose insights, teachings, and collaboration have enriched my understanding and shaped my perspective.

To every person I've crossed paths with, from all walks of life, whose unique experiences and perspectives have broadened my horizons and contributed to my growth as an individual and author.

Lastly, I thank my teenage daughter for being a marvel in my life.

Google, Grammarly, and GPT are also great places to refer to for their vast foundations of knowledge, so thank you all.

Watch out for CS MasterBytes Volume 2 as Your New Compass

With the release of each new CX MasterByte volume, the horizon of possibilities expands, offering fresh insights, deeper wisdom, and boundless growth opportunities. As the CX landscape evolves and customer expectations shift, staying abreast of the latest trends, strategies, and best practices is imperative for success. With each annual update, CX MasterBytes volumes equip readers with the latest tools, methodologies, and case studies to navigate the ever-changing CX terrain. Whether you're a seasoned CX professional or just beginning your journey, buying the annual release ensures that you're armed with the most relevant and up-to-date knowledge to drive meaningful change and deliver exceptional experiences.